A SOCIOLOGICAL APPROACH TO MORALITY

Phillip R. Kunz
Eric M. Jaehne

Brigham Young University

UNIVERSITY
PRESS OF
AMERICA

LANHAM • NEW YORK • LONDON

DEDICATION

Dedicated to our parents who transmitted to us, and to our wives, who assume most of the task of transmitting to our children.

iii

TABLE OF CONTENTS

INTRODUCTION

* * * * *

This paper presents an overview of the area of moral development, with implications derived from a sociological perspective. Probably real solutions to the problems associated with the area of moral development will come from an eclectic approach utilizing the combined knowledge of psychology, sociology, political science, developmental psychology, theology and a host of other disciplines, as well as from a humanistic or secular perspective. Such a total understanding must be preceded by concerted effort in the more specific areas, however. The purpose of this paper is to examine the area of morality from a sociological position, and explicate those areas of moral development which are properly the domain of this perspective.

While we treat the topic from a sociological perspective, we should state that our personal position, as authors, is toward a rather conservative moral position, with some moral absolutes stemming from a religious tradition.

We begin with a statement to the effect that there has been widespread concern over the moral fabric of America and of at least parts of the rest of the world, if not the whole of it. We then explore some of the problems associated with the transmission of moral values as an important segment of the product of socialization, or the manner in which newcomers to a system are made a real part of that system. An explanation of the concept of societies as systems follows.

Socialization and its relationship to moral values is discussed, in terms of societal alternatives which encompass the ranges of behavior presented to an individual as a consequence of being a member of a particular society.

The discussion proceeds with a section on the sources of moral values. Four principle sources are identified and an explanation with examples is presented for each. Individual factors are then elaborated as they pertain to moral behavior. Moral change, or in this case the phenomenon of a perceived "breakdown" of morality, is discussed, with the presentation of some concrete examples both from actual situations and from controlled laboratory experiments.

Positing that there are a number of systems present in any given culture, the process of a system selection is approached. The notions of position and role are dealt with, and the question of moral development is re-approached from the role/system perspective. Situational alternatives, similar to the societal alternatives in function, are proposed as elements in the decision-making process.

The context of the situation, encompassing the "definition of the situation" is explained, along with its consequences for the moral development process. Sanctions and their relationship to the transmission of moral values are the subjects of the next sections. Internalization is reexamined from a sociological point of view.

Several levels of morality are presented, followed by definitions and explanations of the concepts of moral action and prudent action.

The subject is summarized and suggestions formulated in the final section of the paper.

Chapter I

THE MORAL FABRIC

As new words like Watergate, Chappaquiddick, and Abscam have taken their places in the language of many Americans, more and more people are beginning to question the state of the moral fabric of America. Thousands of people have lost many millions of dollars in various scams, schemes, and swindles. As misbehavior occurs in various levels of the social structure, many are led to assert that there has been a diminution of "good behavior."

When such a questioning occurs it may originate from various perspectives. For example the question may stem from a traditional religious-oriented morality, from the new secular morality, or perhaps from one or more of the radical perspectives. What may not be known, however, is whether there has been an actual change in the ratio of "good" and "bad" behavior or only a change in the awareness of that behavior. Or the behavior may go in cycles of better or worse. Yankelovich[1] finds a new human need for self-expression is being linked to an older appreciation of commitment to family and community.

This leads to a major alternative manner in which the problem may be examined. Fewer persons may raise the question in this manner. They may inquire whether the system may only have undergone change and in reality exhibits as much morality now as it ever has in its history. This leads to the question of whether it is possible in retrospect to judge and compare the moral fabric of earlier times and the present. At least one must be very cautious as to the research design which would render such a comparison.

To take this latter position, an extreme position compared with the first, much of this increase of immorality in crime may be due to different reporting practices and better systems of law enforcement and so on. Viewed from this different stance one might argue

---

[1]Daniel Yankelovich, New Rules: Searching for Self-fulfillment in a World Turned Upside Down, Random House, 1981.

1

that in actuality we may be experiencing a period which is more $_2$"moral" than a previous period. Thus, Lauderdale^2 reports that the definition and volume of deviance can change in a system in a manner which is not dependent upon the actions of the deviants, but results from a change in the moral boundaries of society.

For purposes of this work, the assumption will be made that arguments relating to better reporting may have some basis in fact; nevertheless, there still remains a body of facts (which will be elaborated in the course of this discussion) which must be explained and related to the behavior of individual human beings. Do these facts regarding the "immoral" behavior of human beings indicate that there has been a general breakdown of the moral system? This question will be dealt with as part of the larger issue of the development, transmission and perpetuation of moral systems.

The moral system has probably changed in some respects over time. Earlier traditional gemeinschaft societies exhibited more continuity in the values transmitted across generations. More modern industrialized societies have greater discontinuity between the values of one generation and the next.

Certainly one of the most crucial issues in moral development is the concept of transmission, which is to say, "How, and to what extent, are moral values passed to new members of a society?" The concept of transmission implies that there is a near-perfect correlation between the attitudes and beliefs of one generation and those of succeeding generations, and that there is some transmission mechanism or mechanisms which permit or perhaps even cause the moral values to be "passed on" from one generation to the next.

Historically it can be demonstrated that many societies have been able to persist over centuries with little significant variation in the system of morals and values, or other parts of the system as well. Cultures in which this perpetuation of values can be

---

^{2}Pat Lauderdale, "Deviance and Moral Boundaries," American Sociological Review, Vol. 41, August, 1976, pp. 600-676.

detected can serve as "ideal types" in the Weberian[3] sense. Such a perpetuation of values can be found in periods of the histories of Egypt, China, Russia, and many of the pre-Columbian South American Cultures. While some may argue that these people made little contribution to the advancement of humanism, they nevertheless had found ways of transmitting their culture which insured that little change would take place across time. Whether the transmission was purposeful or accidental in such cases is a different kind of problem and will not be discussed here.

On the other end of the continuum are the infrequent examples of culture groups whose most noticeable attribute is a proclivity for change. Some of the early Mongol tribes exhibited an amazing capacity for change and adaptation as they incorporated conquered peoples into their culture and adopted conquered religious and political systems. Transmission of moral values in these kinds of societies is influenced to a large extent by the high rate of movement of other people through the land as they participate on missions of war or commerce. For them adaptation seemed to insure their viability as a power force for a long time. Perhaps the long duration of the Catholic Church is an example of the large amount of adaptation which increases the likelihood of survival of an organization--in this case a religious organization.

Obviously, as cultures of the 1980s are considered, they could be found somewhere toward the end of the continuum toward discontinuity. It probably makes more sense, at this particular stage of development in the social sciences, to speak of an evolutionary, and somewhat gradual but constant, thread of change running through modern cultures. This means that the culture under which children are raised is a continuation of the culture of the parents, with new elements accepted into the culture at differential rates, and from differential sources. Some of this change during the past half century may be seen as revolutionary change. An emergence of a social-secular

---

[3]Max Weber, The Theory of Social and Economic Organization. Edited by Talcott Parsons. New York: Oxford University Press, 1947, p. 13.

ethic seems to have replaced much of the strength of an older Protestant-Puritan-Religious ethic.

Parenthetically, we may digress momentarily to indicate an example of a "functional" culture change. In modern America, with the nuclear family organization, many believe that it is neither practical nor physically feasible for children to take care of their aged parents. Therefore we have seen the proliferation of nursing homes and other places where the old go to live out their remaining years or for some just to die.

This is a clear-cut change from the traditional family arrangement believed by many to have been popular throughout the early history of the United States. In those days, as farmers, Americans could take care of each other. Now, as city-dwellers, and highly mobile ones at that (with nearly one in five families changing residences each year), their loyalties seemingly must be directed in different directions. As a consequence various governmental agencies have been created to perform many of the functions earlier believed to have been filled by the family institution. While some will interpret the proliferation of these agencies and the concomitant decrease in direct family intervention for the elderly as a significant indication of decreasing moral responsibility in which children no longer are concerned with or love their elderly parents, perhaps the phenomenon would better be interpreted as a change brought about by changing mobility patterns, and not an expression of the moral commitment of children towards the care of their aged parents.

Once one accepts the notion that there is in fact a general moral decline, it is easy to accept statements such as the following to be representative of the current trend in moral values in modern America: "Our grandparents called it the Holy Sabbath, our fathers called it the Sabbath, we call it Sunday and our children call it the weekend." Clearly, a concept formerly filled with the multiplicity of religious values implied in the statement is now only an expression of secular practice for many.

By "current trend," it is implied that this is the "perceived" notion of the way in which values are changing. There may be some empirical evidence for believing that way. While the figures indicate that

4

church attendance for some categories of people is somewhat lower now, in reality there has been rather rapid variation in attendance over time for various religious organizations. And in many other areas of behavior there seem to be tendencies to depart from the more traditional methods of behaving--many of these involving moral decisions. So it is this kind of feeling that is at issue in the agitation being experienced by some people as they see their old paths rapidly changing.

Some of this change may occur because of the manner in which it is defined. Let us consider crime for a moment. Hardly anyone would state that crime is not a problem or that criminals show strong signs of moral conviction.

Durkheim makes the point that in the biological area one can define what is pathological only in relation to a given species. He says,

Each species has a health of its own, because it has an average type of its own. Hence, there exists a state of health for the lowest species as well as for the highest. The same principle applies to sociology, although it is most misunderstood here. One should completely abandon the still too widespread habit of judging an institution, a practice or a moral standard as if it were good or bad in itself for all social types indiscriminately.[4]

As Durkheim goes on to discuss crime, he indicates that for almost all people crime would be seen as pathological in society, and yet he points out how crime serves certain functions and may become a source of positive input in society.

In such a case the morality of crime may have to be judged at different levels. We might pursue Durkheim's thinking a little bit more with some current examples of our own making. The first example points out reasons which may result in some differential

---

[4]Emile Durkheim, The Rules of Sociological Method, 8th Edition, Toronto: Collier-MacMillan Canada Ltd., p. 56.

judgment of the strength of values relative to certain areas of crime.

Let us take the case of stereo cassette players for automobiles as a case in point. These have been very "hot items" for young people, and perhaps old as well, which may explain why there have been so many of these items stolen from cars that many insurance companies now specifically exclude stereo cassette players on the automobile insurance policy. Clearly from one position one would argue that it would be very immoral to steal someone else's property. The point that Durkheim might take is that it might be functional for society, or at least certain parts of society, for the stealing to take place. That is, positive good might accrue to someone.

In this case the maker of the stereo player could have a much better business because he is producing more stereos for sale and in turn may be paying more tax money which somehow might benefit society. Perhaps one has to stretch the imagination a good deal to support this line of reasoning. However, to a limited extent, it may be so.

Thus, it may be argued that the general price of the stereo player would preclude a certain segment of society from owning the cassette player. If some members of that financially poorer segment stole the cassette players, some, perhaps most, of those who were able to afford the cassette players and were the rightful owners would replace them either with their own money or by the insurance company settlement, if covered.

If such were to occur, two cassette players would be purchased where only one was purchased without the stealing. That is, a larger segment of society would be served cassette players and the overall profit by the cassette manufacturer would increase to a significant degree. It is possible that the manufacturers could even present their goods to the public in an easy-to-steal form with this in mind.

Likewise, in a more general sense, the high incidence of crime provides employment for detectives, investigators, policemen, lab technicians, and so on. One might argue that if crime were to be "done away with" in the society, then all the expenses associated with that phenomenon would accrue to some other social good. That, of course, is a debatable question. We would not argue that crime is therefore serving the function that nothing else could serve, only that crime is serving a particular type of function which would at least require modification of part of our system if the crime were to suddenly cease.

One might look at accidents as another case in point. In the United States we spend 47 billion dollars[5] each year because of accidents. Part of this expenditure goes to fund various safety committees with their campaigns decrying the wastage of the dollars. Other resources including human life is tragically lost and the suffering of pain and death is great. Safety people indicate that we ought to be more careful because accidents represent wasted money which is not then of value in the economic system. The argument that we make, however, is that the accident does not in and of itself require wasted money, but is only a waste in a relative sense when one considers expenditure for the accidents rather than for other kinds of social goods. Thus, the mere fact that the billions are spent on accidents also means that many people are employed as insurance agents, adjusters, fender menders, doctors, ambulance drivers, and builders, and even members of safety committees. Thus the money which is spent on accidents is not money "down the drain" in terms of the whole economy although for the particular person to whom the accident happens it may seem to be a waste, as it may be similarly judged by those who would have preferred it to have been spent more directly in line with their own interests and needs.

Returning to the crime example, let us conclude for the moment that crime is all bad in spite of the above examples. By whatever standard one measures crime, there is a rather general agreement in American society that the amount of crime has been increasing in the United States, and that the increase in crime is evidence of a general moral decline among the country's inhabitants. Periodically newspaper articles, scientific articles and other pronouncements by public and private individuals point out that crime is reaching staggering proportions and that a national crisis exists as a result of this increase. The

---

[5]"Accidents," Encyclopedia Americana, Vol. 1, 1980, p. 77.

argument is made that crime, as a violation of enacted law upon which people presumably agree, is an affront to society and a general indication of the breakdown of moral standards.

Let us argue for the moment that an increasing amount of crime would be a true indication of lower morality within a society. There exists a problem, then, in that one has to first document the amount of crime to determine whether or not there has been an increase. The amount of crime in society is not really known by anyone. It is true that the FBI Uniform Crime Reports have been utilized by many as an index of major crimes and that these are generally assumed to be correct relative to the amount of crime within a society by the media and by most lay people in particular.

However, much of the crime that is committed within a society can never be really known because of the kinds of detection and reporting methods that are used. Thus, an individual who commits a crime may be observed by no one, and the particular crime that he commits may never come to the attention of the public, or for that matter, even the individual whom the crime is perpetrated against. Thus, an individual may have a considerable amount of his property stolen from him, but may never realize that it is missing or, once finding it missing, he may judge that he had misplaced it or "lost" it when in reality it was stolen. If an individual who commits a crime is detected in that crime by another, that is, if someone observes him in the commission of the crime, there is no guarantee that that commission would be reported to anyone in the justice system, or, for that matter, to anyone else. Thus, there is probably a great amount of activity that would be classified as criminal which goes undetected and there is much crime which, apparently once detected by an individual, still is not reported and therefore does not become part of the official crime statistics.

It is evident from the study done by NORC and by the President's Commission on Law Enforcement and the Administration of Justice that the FBI Uniform Crime Report under-reports certain areas of crime. For example, rape and assault are typically under-reported by the FBI as one compares the studies on victimization

8

with official statistics.[6] From this line of reasoning it may be concluded, first of all, that if crime statistics reported in the media are only rough indications of the real amount of crime, then any dramatic increase in the amount of crime reported may, in fact, not reflect any real difference in the amount of behavior in society, but may occur for other kinds of reasons.

It may be, for example, that an increase in the amount of crime--the "crime-wave" of the front page--results because the police system has become more effective and they are able to detect and book more individuals who have committed crimes. On the other hand, it may also be possible that the increase in the amount of crime occurs merely because there is a change in the reporting procedure within the justice system. That is, acts which were previously reported in one category, or not at all, may suddenly be reported in other categories because of legal prescription or because of administrative decisions, thus increasing the amount of crime. For example, when many states made possession of marijuana a <u>misdemeanor</u>, they experienced a drop in the number of <u>felony</u> drug arrests.

Even if one grants the assumption that the amount of crime is not known but that the real crime detected, the arrests made, the processing of criminals, and so on is increased in a community, one may argue that the increase does not constitute a lower level of morality in the community, but indeed may be a mark of a more moral society rather than a less moral society. One asks, how may this be so? In explaining this, let us assume for a moment that the number of crimes committed over a five-year period does not change in any one year, that is the same number of crimes are actually committed each year. Of all those crimes committed, only a proportion are detected by individuals within the society itself and only a smaller proportion of those that are detected are reported to the police system. At each step in the justice process, there is therefore an attrition of the original number. That is, we start with a basic number of crimes committed, few of these are detected, and even fewer are reported.

---

[6]"Crime," The Encyclopedia of Sociology, Guiford: OPG Reference Publishing, Inc., 1981, pp. 67-68.

There is, then, something within the system which dictates whether someone who detects a crime will or will not actually report it--presumably so that justice may be done. In addition, or course, there is the possibility that the criminal himself will self-report his act, and this frequently happens in certain types of crimes.

Proceeding with the example that the amount of crime is equal over the period of time, let us assume for a moment that suddenly the reported proportion of detected crime significantly increases; that is, more of the crimes committed are now brought to the attention of the police system and therefore enter the stream of the justice system. We may ask what type of occurrence in society might bring about this increase in the reporting of detected crime. This may occur for various reasons such as a religious revival among the people, a dramatic incident in society such as Watergate which pricks the conscience of the people, and so on.

At any rate, with the level occurrence of crime over the years and the sudden increase in the reporting of detected crime, it may be argued that there is an increase in the moral level of people in society. Thus what appears to be a contradiction in terms, that is, an increase in the crime rate indicates an increasingly moral society, may actually be so because it comes from a people who have suddenly seen the necessity of reporting the detected crime, that is, whose moral position is that the good of society is best met by their reporting what they know about crime.

Note, then, that the increase in the crime rate has occurred not because there has been any change in the amount of commission of crime, but only in the reporting of the crime committed. Thus the increase in rate which some would attribute to be a less moral society may indeed be just the reverse, that is, more people in the society are morally concerned about the society and therefore are willing to aid the justice system in bringing about more law and order.

Another very vital factor which has recently been demonstrated by the President's Commission on Law Enforcement and the Administration of Justice, but which has been recognized by Sociologists in other contexts for many years is that the particular age structure of a society may account for much of the variability in the amount of crime, because certain types of crime are generally committed by people within particular age compositions. Thus the President's Commission indicated that in 1965 more than 44 percent of all persons arrested for forceable rape, more than 39 percent of the robbery, and over 26 percent of all the homicide and aggravated assault were committed by people within the 18-24 age group category. Because of the changing age structure in the United States resulting from the baby boom in the post-war years of the Second World War, there are more youthful people within the society which in turn increases the base from which criminals would result in the early youth categories. "Commission studies based on 1960 arrest rates indicate that between 1960 and 1965 about 40 to 50 percent of the total increase in the arrests reported by the UCR could have been expected as a result of increase in population and changes in the age composition of the population."[7]

The importance of the age structure in the population is also found in other areas which we associate with the general moral structure. Thus England and Kunz found that increases in the divorce rate may in part be explained by the age composition of the society. Because of the importance of the concept we quote at length.

> Suppose a community (i.e., a new suburban development) has 10,000 married couples, 1,000 of whom obtain divorces in a given year. The same community has very few single people of marriageable age, hence, there are only 1,000 marriages that same year. The marriage to divorce rate would be 1. This could be interpreted as meaning that marital relationships are in serious trouble in this community. In fact, if the popular interpretation is employed, we would say that every marriage entered into will end in divorce. The interpretation is misleading because a very large population of married, divorceable couples is compared with a small population of single, marriageable couples.

---

[7]Robert W. Winslow, Crime in a Free Society, San Diego: Dickenson Publishing Company, Inc., 1968, p. 54.

Another hypothetical community of 100,000 perhaps with a large university, where there are large numbers of single people of marriageable age, can also be examined. Suppose there are the same number divorces as in the above example: 1,000. There are, however, 10,000 marriages. The marriage to divorce reates would be 10 to 1, which would be much more favorable than the first example even though the <u>crude divorce rates would be equal</u> in both examples. . . .

Sometimes the particular methodology is also very influential of what might be reported. A major problem with refining divorce rate is that it is insensitive to variations in the age compositions of the married population. It is commonly reported that younger married persons have a greater probability of divorce than do older married persons. Two populations of married persons may appear to have very different tendencies to divorce, not because there is greater cultural acceptance of divorce, but simply because they have very different age structures. . . .

For example suppose we have three areas: Penoso, Mediania, and Felicidad each with one million inhabitants. Penoso has a refined divorce rate of 33.10 per 1,000 married women. Mediania has a rate of 16.05. Felicidad has a rate of 6.94. Consequently, the local social work agencies in Penoso conclude that marriage in their area is under severe stress and begin a campaign to remedy the problem. They adopt a program that has been employed in Felicidad with apparent success.

Felicidad is one with a relatively old population of married women.

Now suppose we survey the divorced women in each of the three communities and discover that the frequency of divorce by the age of the wife is distributed as in Table 2.

12

TABLE 1
MARRIED WOMEN FOR
HYPOTHETICAL POPULATIONS

	Penoso Area I	Mediania Area II	Felicidad Area III
14-19	170,000	10,000	2,000
20-24	210,000	20,000	4,000
25-29	240,000	50,000	6,000
30-34	190,000	100,000	12,000
35-39	95,000	200,000	24,000
40-44	47,000	240,000	47,000
45-49	24,000	200,000	95,000
50-54	12,000	100,000	190,000
55-59	6,000	50,000	240,000
60-64	4,000	20,000	210,000
65+	2,000	10,000	170,000

TABLE 2
NUMBER OF DIVORCES IN
EACH AGE CATEGORY

	Penoso Area I	Mediana Area II	Felicidad Area III	Age Specific Rates
14-19	94,432	5,496	1,099	54.96
20-24	91,287	8,694	1,739	43.47
25-29	73,800	15,375	1,845	30.75
30-34	41,895	22,050	2,646	22.05
35-39	18,392	38,720	4,646	19.36
40-44	6,923	35,352	6,923	14.73
45-49	2,794	23,280	11,058	11.64
50-54	948	7,900	15,010	7.90
60-64	153	764	8,022	3.82
65+	44	221	3,757	2.21

	Total Divorces	Refined Rate
Penoso	330,984	37.10
Mediania	160,488	16.05
Felicidad	69,369	6.94

The computation of the proportion of divorces
to the number of married women in each age

13

category is the same for all three
communities. The row labeled "Age-Specific
Rates" is the proportion multiplied by 1,000.
Hence, all of the variation in the refined
divorce rates of the three areas is due to
the differences in their age distributions.[8]

One could go on, of course, to draw the specific
problem out in this case, that is, that increasing
amount of divorce in a society is also indicative of a
lowering moral standard. As may be demonstrated by the
material above, however, an increase in the divorce
rate may in fact be reflective of only a change in the
age structure or of some other kinds of factors.

Upon development of a new oil field, there are
often great population increases in nearby towns.
Crime seems to increase almost at once and the blame
generally goes to the oil field workers who are seen as
riff-raff. What is generally not understood is that
most of the oil workers are young and in the age
category where high amounts of certain types of crime
are evident; thus, it may be the changing age structure
that increases the crime rather than the oil field
workers per se.

One may argue that an increase in the amount of
divorce may in fact demonstrate a more moral society.
The reasoning of that statement is difficult for many
to follow. Thus, an increase in the amount of divorce
sometimes results from a change in position in a
society. The change is to a position which treats the
importance of the individual and his well-being as more
important than the relationship between a couple.
Thus, if an individual is saddled with a mate who is
causing all kinds of difficulties for him or her and as
a consequence one has an unhappy marriage, to allow
them to divorce and seek a better marriage partner
somewhere else may be a higher moral order.

The research tends to indicate that the marriages
which occur after the first divorce are generally more
happy, so this position argues that the individuals are
in a better circumstance. The position of the children

---

[8]J. Lynn England and Phillip R. Kunz, "Age
Specific Divorce Rates," Journal of Marriage and the
Family, Vol. 37, February, 1975, pp. 40-46.

14

and society in general relative to the divorce may be argued further, but will not be done here. Suffice it to say that the end result of the divorce in one situation is much like that of crime, that is, the change is the rate per se does not always constitute ipso facto evidence of a change in the moral position or moral structure or moral fiber of a society. This line of reasoning does not discount the high cost to society of high divorce rates. The effect of divorce on children, other family members, and society in general is quite evident.

In a recent study (1974) by Dertke, Penner, and Ulrich, an experimental situation was set up where shoplifting acts were perpetrated in a very obvious way for the purpose of determining how many of the shoplifters would be reported and confirmed by witnesses. The incident of reporting and confirmation would presumably be visualized as an act of morality or at least an outgrowth of an adequate moral value system. The findings were that blacks were reported and confirmed more often than whites, although the thefts were perpetrated equally by white male, white female, black male, and black female confederates. In a real sense, then, the act of reporting the shoplifting incident is influenced by the race of the violator more than by the incident itself. Thus, one's ethnic origin is a better predictor than the general societal moral value teachings.[9]

Another example of how an increase in crime rate may be attributed to artifacts and not to any changing moral position is that of an increase in the number of felonies as opposed to misdemeanors arising from an increase in value of the product stolen. For example, if we were to take the case of the stereo cassette players for automobiles which we have discussed earlier and assume for a moment that they cost $5 beneath the limit for a misdemeanor, that is, all of the cases of the stolen cassettes would be classified legally as misdemeanors and therefore probably would not really be brought to the attention of the public; if, however, in an inflationary period in society the cost of the

---

[9]Max C. Dertke, Louis A. Penner, and Kathleen Ulrich, "Observer's Reporting of Shoplifting as a Function of Thief's Race and Sex," Journal of Social Psychology, Vol. 94, 1973, pp. 213-221.

stereo increases to $75 or $100 or at least a few dollars above the limit defining a misdemeanor as opposed to a felony, then all of these cases become felonies rather than misdemeanors and would show up as an increase in the overall crime rate as far as most people are concerned, and would probably be treated as such by the media. Thus there would be a tremendous increase in the seriousness and amount of crime without any change occurring in the actual behavior of the citizenry. The increase would result solely from the inflationary trend on the product sold.

Clearly, more than perception is at issue as there have been some changes in the way people really behave. Nudity in public, once proscribed, is now the sine qua non of some ocean beaches. Abortion, previously seldom even discussed, is now advertised in the media on billboards. The question is, is there a concomitant change in attitude which goes along with the more visible changes? The almost inescapable conclusion is that, yes, there have been some basic changes in attitude and behavior as the legal status on abortion has changed. We sometimes hear people say that you can't legislate morality. The court decision regarding abortion has appeared to influence basic abortion attitudes for many people in America. Of course many Americans take a very strong position against abortion. The abortion issue is divisive and that divisiveness has certainly increased since the court decision.

What, then, is at work behind the scenes which could cause this kind of change in attitude from generation to generation? Are there specific mechanisms for the transmission of morality, or is it left to chance? Does such change occur, at the link between one generation and another, or does it occur at some point in time irrespective of and unrelated to generation? Implied in the discussion as many people interpret it, is the notion that it is clearly a generation linkage problem. As these people see it, the problem of transmission breakdown (inadequate transmission), is a failure of parents to teach their children. This point of view is summed up by the phrase, "There are no delinquent children, only delinquent parents." Thus, some judges want to sentence the children's parents, not the children. Holding to that opinion implies that one has arrived at a de facto answer to the two questions stated above. If one views parents as being responsible for the change in moral behavior because of inadequate

16

parentage, then one has concluded that (1) there are specific mechanisms for change, and (2) change occurs at the link between one generation and another. Further, they have decided that the specific mechanisms for transmission and change are found in the family, with the parent in primary control of that link.

Allowing that the family plays some significant part in the transmission process, it must also be recognized that there may be other mechanisms involved as well. The extent of each of these involvements is an empirical question. Similarly, change is ubiquitous, so that it becomes naive to speak of one point in time as being totally inclusive of the change. Certainly children may change from or be different from their parents, and much change will be found at generation linkage points, but all the while the children are changing the parents and grandparents may also be changing to a greater or lesser extent as the society changes. Usually those who decry the failure of parents to teach their children do not perceive the change in all parts of society but only in breakdown as it impinges on the children.

It is interesting that while some see the young involved in change and assume the elderly to be resistant to change, the older people have undergone very large amounts of change, as empirical evidence demonstrates. The period of time elapsed during the older people's lifetime has included vast amounts of change in almost all areas of social and technological life.

Chapter II

TRANSMISSION OF MORALITY

Before proceeding to a presentation of specific cases and analyses, and to facilitate understanding of problems, certain terms and concepts must be defined so that the reader will understand how we have used these terms. To this point the words morality and transmission have been used with the understanding that everyone has some kind of working definition of the words, though the definitions may cover a wide spectrum of meaning. Since definition without a corresponding conception of the context within which the definition operates would be useless, we will preface these definitions with a discussion of the social and sociological contexts of morality and transmission of morality.

For the purposes of our discussion, human beings will be treated as members of systems, specifically, human society is seen as a system. Herbert Spencer, one of the early pioneers of sociology, viewed human societal systems as having many of the same general kinds of characteristics as organismic systems. Several of his students and other sociologists of his period took a more literal approach than Spencer, and began formulating complex paradigms in which each segment of society was compared to a part of an organism, e.g., the brain would find its counterpart in society in the "elites" who make decisions for the whole system.

Spencer never intended a literal approach to his conceptualization, since he used it primarily as a means of conceptualizing the complex entity known as society. It helped him to think of the various parts of societies as having some contribution to make to the larger group, and to that extent his view can be useful. While the organismic view of society has never really been widely accepted, its contribution to the notion of systems has been helpful. Today many of the elements which make up a society have distinct functions which they perform and which are vital to the ongoing processes of the society.

Society today, then, can be viewed as a system, or even many diverse systems, for several reasons, although this work is not an attempt to prove systems theory. It is merely pointed out that many properties of systems operate in societies and that a systems perspective can be useful in dealing with problems of a societal nature. Like other systems (e.g., mechanical, organismic), societies are engaged in goal-fulfilling behavior, which is to say that the activities within societies are seldom random, but rather occur for a reason. Change is an integral part of society, especially as societies are viewed as open systems, i.e., open to new input from external sources. Within the systems perspective, societies are seen as being greater than the sum of their parts.

It follows, then, that when a society is referred to as a social system, it refers in part to the fact that social life involves a commitment to a set of rules, and an obligation to behave in a manner which is beneficial to the system or at least in a manner which doesn't threaten the system. Accordingly, those individuals within a system who proceed to violate the rules of the system are labeled as being deviant. We will consider later on the implications of deviance. Within a system, Durkheim argued for the positive functions of deviance, as have others since. Suffice it to say here that only as deviance concerns areas defined as being in the moral realm are we concerned with it in this paper.

Within the framework of a systems approach to social life, the question of maintenance must be dealt with. As noted above, there is an obligation to behave in socially acceptable ways, but this obligation and commitment to a set of rules may be explicit and conscious or only implied and for most members of society, unconscious. Knowing this, how can one explain the fact that societies are able to persist over long periods of time approaching 200 years in the case of America, and in a significant number of ancient societies over many centuries (e.g., China and Egypt); how can they persist and yet still retain many of the values and principles developed early in their history? Sociologists have identified several elements involved in this maintenance process.[10] One element with

---

[10] D. F. Aberle, "Functional Requisites of a Society," in System Change and Conflict, edited by N. J. Demerath and R. A. Peterson. New York: The Free Press, 1967.

particular significance for the topic of moral development is a process known as socialization.

Briefly, socialization can be described as that process by which new members of society, or a system, are taught the ways of the system. Such teaching involves not only the transmission of knowledge of how the society operates but the motivational force necessary to get the people within the system to behave within the acceptable limits of the prescribed norms. These norms include both folkways, or ways of doing things which have no moral significance, and the mores, which involve strong moral demands. Children may be seen as actors who have come in to a play in the middle of the second act. It is the duty of part of the rest of the actors in the production to "fill in" the newcomers and explain both what has gone before and the parts which they will be expected to play.

An understanding of the concept of socialization reinforces the notion that the family is a vitally important part in the life of individual actors (people). The family is a very significant force in the socialization of children and of their subsequent morality. While it is true that some people can and do change their lives to become something entirely different from the thing they were socialized to become, it remains that the family can impart certain long-lasting and powerful characteristics to its children. The family is still recognized by almost all sociologists as the unit with the primary responsibility of socializing the young.

It is apparent, then, that socialization is important for many reasons. One of the primary functions of socialization is related to the standing a person will have in his system. Until a person has an understanding of and a willingness to abide by the rules of a system, he will be considered by that system to be less than a full-fledged member, and may even be perceived as a threat to the system. Unwillingness to so abide can have profound consequences for the individual. He may feel pressure to withdraw from participation in the activities in the system, or he may be forcibly ejected. In some cases the ejection may be final and complete as in the case of legal executions, where a system rids itself permanently of a disobedient member.

As children grow into adulthood, they are subjected successively to the influences of a number of institutions whose purpose it is to socialize them. The family is the first institution, and soon thereafter the child finds himself in school, where he is formally socialized (or at least an attempt is made to socialize him). Through the effects of these and other institutions and elements of societies, children are taught (or at least exposed to) what is expected of them in general terms, and they are exposed to social pressure to conform to the expectations. While there is a separation of church and state in America, everyone doesn't think the school is exempt from teaching moral values. Cogdell argues that

> If our schools do not teach students the importance of keeping one's word, of abiding by covenants, of paying one's debts, of steady habits of work and thrift, then the underlying foundation of trust and confidence, which must undergird all relationships in a civilized society, will erode and finally collapse.[11]

As a consequence, most societies have "children" and "adults" whose positions are defined in the legal statutes or by long-standing custom. The titles "child" and "adult" reflect the degree to which the individual is expected to adhere to the rules of society. Adults are expected to know and obey the rules, and children are given somewhat more freedom to disobey. This leeway in expectations is also extended, to some extent, to the newcomer or immigrant to the system. These two groups, the infant and the immigrant, are important to the system in a unique way since without them the system would perish. This perhaps accounts for the differential assignment of responsibilities. In any event, both of these groups are expected to eventually learn and live the rules, even if they do nothing else. Frequently, proscribed behavior is tolerated for a time when the offender is an obvious newcomer to the system. One of the problems experienced by our society is that we do not have clear-cut, fast passage from the child stage to the adult stage. Adolescence is a time of

---

[11]Gaston Cogdell, "Religion and Moral Education," The Humanist, November/December, 1978, p. 22.

status change which lasts very long in western societies compared with the practices of some societies. An adolescent is neither a child nor an adult and the compliance patterns are not really very clear as a result.

In any system, the rules are of vital importance. The alternative to government by law is government by the whim of the powerful or government by mob. Of these three, government by law seems to be the most preferred and most productive. The rules of a system become important as system members become socialized. As adults, the individuals may find that the rules take on value simply because they are rules, rather than for any actual importance to the system. At that point the rules have become institutionalized. The United States abounds with such rules or norms, and every now and then one of them is enforced and a test case results and the rule may be found to be unconstitutional.

An example of this can be found in a little town in California. Founded by Methodists, the town has been historically a "dry" town (regarding the sale of alcoholic beverages). One day one of the grocery stores in the town decided to sell beer. When taken to court, the law was struck down, and an institutionalized rule that had stood for over one hundred years was changed. The point is that all of that time the residents had obeyed the rule without stopping to consider the constitutionality of it.

Underlying these rules or norms are found the moral values, which, in addition to spawning the rules, are also capable of giving an aura of "rightness" or "wrongness" to specific as well as general areas of behavior. Clearly, though, the process is two-way. While the moral values frequently result in the codification of rules as in the California town the rules can sometimes be responsible for things becoming accepted as being "moral." The idea of having two very different sources for moral values suggest wide-ranging implications.

In the past in America, the moral values predominated in many spheres of life. For example, swearing has traditionally been held to be a less-than-desirable way of behaving, and until recently this moral edict operated to keep swearing and "swear words' out of the media and off the movie screens. Through a complex and not completely understood process, the media and the "silver screen" now seem to be involved in the creation of moral values. Instead of the society dictating with its unwritten moral values what should and should not be allowed on the air (screen), the situation seems to have been reversed, with moral values in individual persons being in part a result of the input from such external sources as movies, television and books.

The foregoing is not meant to be an indictment of Hollywood or an investigation into the content and effect of movies, it is merely to illustrate some of the changes and contradictions which exist in the area of our moral sphere. In this context, however, it will be interesting to see the eventual outcome of some of the new interpretations of the law, especially the abortion laws. Abortion has become a morally viable option to birth for some now that it has become legally available. The law is differentially accepted by various segments of society. It is an intriguing question as to the kinds and amounts of power involved in the change of a moral value. There is currently a great deal of effort being expended to reduce the availability of abortion.

Recent reports indicate that there is wide-spread dissatisfaction with the highly-touted vasectomy approach to birth control, and this may be an indication of stronger action in the future to prevent people from making certain decisions regarding their own bodies. What this has to do with moral development is simply this: it is clear that there is a relationship between law and morality, and empirical research is needed to indicate the relative strength of this relationship and to discover the ways and means by which they influence one another.

From the above it is clear that there is a relationship between the laws and rules of specific societies and the way people in those societies feel about certain things with regards to right and wrong. Elaborating on this notion, it is evident that there is a connection between the beliefs of a society and the behavior of its members. for example, consider a headhunter in the darkest jungles of New Guinea. When such a person becomes "insane," would we expect him to go about pretending that he is Napoleon? For simple and yet far-reaching reasons, we should not. The principle reason is that he has never heard of Napoleon, and this is an illustration of the general

24

principle that human behavior is a matter of picking and choosing from among the alternatives presented by the social system of which each individual is a member.

It is frequently stated that men are "products of their environment," and to some extent this is true, especially when seen in the light of the above example. On the other hand, it must be remembered that most environments offer a wide variety of behaviors, so that it becomes inaccurate to assume that a given set of environmental factors is capable of producing only one kind of individual. This idea of societal alternatives will be discussed in more detail later. But for now it will suffice to state and illustrate the principles involved.

It may be helpful at this point to draw an analogy with something familiar to help in understanding the principle of societal alternatives. The act of communicating, as practiced by human beings, is totally dependent on the existence and mutual acceptance of symbols. Symbols may be words, signs, gestures, expressions, etc. While the notion of there having been an actual tower of Babel is intuitively unreasonable to many people, the explanation of the chaos which resulted from the sudden and instantaneous confusion of dialects is completely understandable. Americans traveling abroad are continually amazed that the natives are unable to understand English no matter how slowly or loudly it is spoken to them. They would find, however, that certain symbols, like a "clenched fist" or a "dirty look," are almost always instantly translated into whatever language is being used. The point is that without a common backlog of mutually held ideas and symbols, communication is impossible.

Similarly, human behavior is completely random and largely meaningless without the explanatory context of a social system. Miner points out the absurdity of trying to understand what is going on as people behave without the "glasses" of a knowledge of the social system under which the subjects are operating.[12]

In communicating, whether people use words or gestures, they are thinking in terms of the symbolic

---

[12]Horace Miner, "Body Ritual Among the Nacirema," _American Anthropologist_, Vol. 58, June, 1956.

meaning of their sounds and movements. In behavior, people are basically assumed to be imitators of what they have seem before, although sometimes they are able to combine two or more previously observed behaviors and come up with what looks like a new behavior. Some studies which have attempted to demonstrate that children imitate parents, however, have not accomplished what they set out to prove. High correlation between behavior of parents and behavior of children may be children imitating parents, parents imitating children, or both parents and children imitating someone else. There is the additional possibility that similar behavior may be a result of both parents and children emitting like behavior with very different underlying motives. Most previous studies on imitation have not accounted for these alternate possibilities.

Nevertheless, imitation is an important factor in the development of the human personality. A study of extremely isolated human beings has indicated that society is an absolutely essential factor in the development of "human" types of behavior patterns. This study dealt with persons who had been almost totally neglected and isolated from birth until middle childhood (one had lain, since her illegitimate birth, in an attic where only her most basic needs were met, i.e., food, diaper changes with an absolute minimum of human contact in the form of loving, talking, holding, etc. Indeed, children frequently die as a result of this kind of emotional neglect even though their physical needs are being met) When found, the children were unable to engage in any distinctly "human" patterns of behavior, neither moving nor making any understandable gestures. Only after years of care and concern in institutional settings were some of the neglected children able to become functioning members of society. Other achieved some level of improvement but remained in a retarded condition for the rest of their lives.[13]

Clearly, then, interaction with other people is a necessity for the learning of human patterns of behavior. The logical conclusion from this assumption

---

[13]Kingsley Davis, "Final Note on a Case of Extreme Isolation," American Journal of Sociology, Vol. 52, 1947.

is that moral values, like behavior patterns, are also functions of the interaction of people. We can conclude that in some way these moral values are transmitted from one person to the next, and from one generation to the next. Making this conclusion suggests some far-reaching (and for some people possibly threatening) implications. First of all, there can be no logical notion of an "absolute" morality, or a system of "absolute" rights and wrongs (leaving for the moment the various religious approaches to this question). This means that the concentration camp guards who actually pulled the triggers and dropped the gas pellets were no more "guilty" of a moral offense than were the American cavalrymen who trained their Hotchkiss guns on unarmed women and children at the Indian massacre at Wounded Knee. In the cold, piercing light of history, these men come up looking evil, but at the time they were doing their duty as their society expected them to do.

To briefly discuss the religious point of view, it seems that the only way an absolute morality could be defended would be to propose that God has some set of rules which he expects people to follow. As people become aware of these rules through one means or another, they then become bound to follow them. It is not logical to suppose that God will extract some form of punishment from those who never heard of his rules. This, then, is a definition and as such is not arguable. As sociologists and as concerned human beings, however, our task must be to understand the process by which morality is transmitted and changed. Without that knowledge society is bound to repeat the mistakes of the past as change occurs under its own power. Without knowledge of the specifics of morality, sometimes the hands of the religionists would be tied as they follow their common sense. Their courses of action may not achieve the expected results. Indeed, Jarvis found that religious education is a poor transmitter of moral values.[14] While an individual, from a religious perspective, may have a "knowledge of moral absolutes," they are not available for empirical demonstration. Such positions must be accepted by "faith" in the system. That is not to argue that such

---

[14]Peter Jarvis, "Religious Education as a Vehicle for Moral Education?" Journal of Moral Education, Vol. 2, No. 1, 1972.

a postion is wrong, but only that it must be outside the realm of science.

From a sociological perspective one would make the assumption that morality could be considered as an absolute only within a cultural context, and then only as the cultural norms prescribe. That is, one would not argue that moral positions are universal, but only relative to particular situations within particular cultures. That is not to say, however, that two or more cultures may not maintain the same position relative to particular moral values, and the mode of behavior for individuals in particular situations, but these similar positions would still be specific to the particular culture involved. For example, while there is a wide-spread belief in the universality of the incest prohibition, there are differential definitions of who it applies to, and while not generally discussed, considerable evidence of its violation.

While it may be determined that a cultural definition, in general, defines killing as wrong, at the same time the culture prescribes times and situations where the taking of the life of another person may not only be permissible but indeed may be mandatory. Thus, in times of war one may become a hero for ending a number of lives in the enemy camp. Or the law may prescribe that a person be put to death for a certain type of offense or violation within the system. The "hangman" or member of a "firing squad" is not faulted for his legal act.

Within the same culture several legal systems and moral positions may be simultaneously held by the group. Thus, legally a person may not be executed until he has had due process of law and has undergone various tests within the court system. But in the same society, under most unusual wartime conditions, a person in command may unilaterally make the judgment to execute a member of his own forces in the name of the good of the system.

Within a culture where moral positions are specified it should also be recognized that constant changes take place and that a position denoting high morality at one point in time may not be so defined at another point in time. Thus, one finds that behavior such as particular types of dances which were believed to be immoral by some segments of the society several

28

decades ago are now accepted and fashionable. Some professions such as law and medicine were determined by some to be immoral at some point in time and are now acceptable and fashionable. The same may occur with other modes of behavior within the society.

Chapter III

SITUATIONAL MORALITY

One of the problems in treating the level of moral development or morality in the society is that one may approach the problem of moral development from several logical positions, or using several methodological techniques. Thus, we may ask persons how they would judge themselves in moral terms as measured against some absolute standard which we call to their attention. We may ask them to make some sort of self-declaration of moral position relative to others of their colleagues, or we may use rather indirect techniques of measuring morality. Experimental situations may be utilized where the moral position is exhibited by behavior of the subjects and the moral position of society may be ascertained by generalization to it from the experimental results. Generally, as morality is concerned, one assumes that the morality of an individual pervades through all areas of his social behavior and indeed would be relevant in all situations. Thus it is assumed that if a person is trustworthy he would be trustworthy at all times and in all situations. Frequently, as adults teach youth, they stress that once one has given his word he ought to fulfill his part of the agreement. Even that, however, is really specific to a situation, as all adults will later teach.

We may begin by telling children that if one agrees to do something, he must do it because that is the right thing to do. Later on in the socialization process we teach the child alternatives, or tell him of occasions where that type of behavior may not be appropriate, but indeed may be very much inappropriate. Parents who teach their children not to let strangers into their house in the absence of their parents soon realize if their children are perceptive such an instruction is not very useful. Such a child may indeed ask a question immediately such as "Well, what if the house is on fire and the fireman comes to the door, but I don't know him?" or "What if my little sister is choking to death and the ambulance comes, shall I let the attendant in the house?" The obvious answer would be, "Of course, but that is a different situation." The child soon learns that life is composed of many different situations. An individual in a position who is defining what correct behavior would be for him has the task of defining the correct moral behavior within some set of standards. Obviously, if he makes the wrong choice, he is taking a somewhat low-level moral position. The choice, however, may not be obvious to him at times. Thus, perhaps some of the people caught up in Watergate were really doing what they believed at the time to be the right thing to do in view of the circumstances. The war trials following the Second World War point to this very type of problem. Thus, many of those on trial believed they were doing the right thing by following orders. At least "at the time" they thought they were correct.

One of the difficulties in determining the correct moral behavior is the problem associated with much of what we do in the human enterprise. The problem of defining reality after the fact is generally quite easy for most people. We make judgments of an individual which may or may not be right, but once an individual has acted in a particular way so that his attention is called to the public or other notice, and then we are called upon to indicate the kind of relationship that we had with the individual, it is easy to redefine our earlier experience to make him the kind of individual that history has now shown him to be.

We see, therefore, a young man who crawls up into a tower in Texas and begins to indiscriminately shoot at passers-by. Individuals who knew him closely were aghast at his behavior and could not understand why he would have done such a thing. In an effort to make this understanding more complete, reporters then go to friends and acquaintances of the young man, asking what kind of person he was. Now, knowing all his bad behavior in public, they redefine their own experiences with him and start to remember the aggression which he showed in elementary school or other kinds of characteristics which would be in harmony with his current behavior.

The problem, of course, is to be able to predict beforehand that that individual was that sort of person. Generally people do not do very well at prediction. This prediction business is really the problem of parole boards, criminologists, supervisors, employers, personnel managers, and so on. All kinds of people have to make judgments of others' behavior in order to predict how they will succeed in a given position.

Individuals view themselves as honest and as a consequence may agree to subscribe to a set of rules and principles which proscribe dishonesty. Thus, in an education situation students generally agree to not cheat and to maintain an honest position relative to their work. Numerous studies, however, have determined that cheating is largely determined by the availability of means for cheating and learning the techniques. Likewise, one would probably add the pressures which induce an individual to take a chance of being cast out of such a system because of cheating. Generally these studies show that students cheat on examinations, papers, and in other circumstances as they believe they will get by with it. Even in institutions in our society which we assume to be the most moral, such as a military institution where honor and honesty are much discussed, there is periodically an outbreak of cheating following which society questions the morality and the system that would permit young people to be socialized in a nonmoral manner. Generally blame is focused on the parents who failed to transmit moral behaviors, or on some other institution other than the one making the judgment.

As the problem of morality is examined, we may look at other cases to determine that the behavior an individual emits is most often related to his position within the system. Thus, we find ample evidence that one's standard on the environmental issues is largely relevant to his position vis-a-vis the specific environmental issues. Thus, one who maintains his livelihood through the steel industry would not be dismayed at pollution rising from the steel industry, but may selectively be in favor of other environmental issues that do not touch upon his own life. Likewise, an individual who may be very concerned with the large amount of the fuel consumed by large luxury cars may at the same time be quite willing to run the air-conditioner in his office on rather marginal occasions.

Some research has even indicated that persons who are most suspect of having "no morals" are often most adamant about enforcing the very rules relative to those morals. For example, in a study of nudist camps it has been determined that the public in general looks upon the members of a nudist society as having rather low sexual morals. The members of the nudist camp, however, set rather stringent rules as regards sex. For example, they do not permit excessive photography

33

on the part of their members; they have certain implicit norms against staring, all of which are quite contrary to what the public in general assumes to be the facts concerning such situations. So the deviant in that case has really taken the norms of the greater culture and adapted them to his own society, not casting them aside, but rather enforcing certain ones with a more stringent attitude than occurs in the society which is castigating him for his membership in the nudist camp.

It is apparent, then, from a sociological perspective, that it does little practical good to speak of moral absolutes, for a person becomes subject to moral values only as he becomes aware of them, and he becomes aware of them only as they are part of the social system into which he is socialized. This isn't to argue that people do not have moral absolutes to guide their lives and from which to judge others. Even so, after a person has become aware of such norms, there is no assurance that he will comply with them. For example, an archaeologist may familiarize himself with the practices of ancient cultures, like Carthage, but he will feel no compulsion to sacrifice his children to pagan idols just because the Carthagenians did. Closer to home, people who are aware of the way children and young people were exploited in America's past are not therefore motivated to exploit their own children.

From the above it is clear that awareness of the existence of certain moral values is a necessary but not sufficient condition for obedience to those same values. Similarly, there is another necessary but not sufficient condition for obedience and that is that the person feel some compulsion, either external or internal, to obey. This element of morality will be given extensive treatment further on.

Chapter IV

SOURCES OF MORAL VALUES

It has been shown that people can be viewed as members of societies and that these societies can be viewed as systems. Further it seems evident that within each system there is a set of moral values, which is to say that certain things are considered to be right and other things are held to be wrong. It is appropriate here to examine some of the origins and meanings of moral values. Four basic areas are identified and discussed in the following pages which seem to be able to initiate and perpetuate moral values.

In almost all societies, religion is a rich source of moral values, indeed, as Durkheim pointed out, one of the chief attributes and duties of a religion is to define for its adherents the difference between the sacred and the profane. A moment's reflection will make it obvious that that is something that religion does very well, and in many cases, religion is the only thing which can apply a label to a particular type of behavior. Religion in America has provided everything from standards outlining what is and what is not appropriate sexual behavior to mottos for coins.

A second source is tradition, which functions in much the same way as religion. The essence of tradition is that its origins are unclear through the mists of time, and therefore could be originally either the result of religious influences or secular practices. Under the general heading of tradition is custom. Once a thing has become a custom it may become an immoral act to violate it simply because it is a custom, rather than for any practical reason.

A third source of moral values is for immigrant groups to bring with them their own moral values some of which may be slowly adopted by the native population. This importation, then, could be either gradual and unconscious or forced and relatively rapid. Such an influx of moral change may arise within a rapidly growing organization from its incoming members who bring old moral values and which the organization can not socialize them rapidly enough to maintain separateness from these new values.

Finally, a fourth method is obvious as it is observed that many moral values in any given system will be the result of practical considerations, many of which will be given status in an explicit manner through the legal system.

We have briefly listed some of the basic sources of moral values in a system; this will be followed with an elaboration of each element. It will be obvious to even the most casual observer that religion and the moral values it perpetuates are still relevant in most societies of the world. Even in societies which are blatantly anti-religious (e.g., The Soviet Union, The People's Republic of China, and so on) many of the formerly religiously-affiliated practices and customs have been continued in different clothing. There are emminently practical reasons for some of them to be carried on. For example, the concept of marriage is now a legal entity where it had been largely religious or (in earlier uses) political. The complex of problems and regulations associated with the marriage state dictate that some kind of formal arrangement be made and recognized by both the state and other people. State-directed debasement of marriage and family were soon found to be a problem for the USSR. They have since attempted to re-establish the importance of marriage.

Even though it may be argued that religious values do not have the daily, forceful impact they once had, they make themselves felt in other ways. People cover their faces and even walk backwards sometimes when entering theaters which are showing X-rated movies because of the moral values associated with sexual behavior. The obvious explanation for this type of behavior would be to attribute it to embarrassment or "social pressure," but the root cause is the fact that certain things are still tainted by the notion of immorality, and these old notions die hard (by way of explanation, the word "notion" is used here to convey the sense of concept, or idea, and is not used disparagingly or smugly). The above kinds of embarrassed behavior are typical in a large city, where more deviance is tolerated. The existence and patrons of X-rated movie houses are seen as being deviant (different), but not necessarily terribly immoral.

In contrast to that situation is the situation which can occur in a smaller town. Small towns are traditionally known (and in some quarters, feared) as the last bastions of the old order. Recently in a small town in a Western state, (where a large percentage of the population are mine workers) raging controversy was fired by the decision of a local theater owner to exhibit pornographic movies in his theater. The theater was picketed, theater patrons were photographed as a deterrent to attendance, and in general the situation became an uproar. Legal action was taken and the case went to the State Supreme Court before an agreement was reached.

Similarly, another small town (with a high percentage of religious people) forced the closure of a "massage parlor" in a matter of weeks through legal action. In cities, massage parlors, Turkish baths, and steam rooms are commonplace. The difference seems to be that in small, rural towns religion is a part of the lives of more people than it is in a big city.

Interestingly, most organized religions generally find agreement in at least one area, and that is the area of sexual conduct. Religions are generally united in the proscription of certain sex practices and attitudes, e.g., premarital intercourse, homosexuality, and sexual activity in general which constitutes a departure from the more "traditional" forms approved by the religious community. Indeed one of the most shocking developments (to many people at least) in the area of morality in recent years has been the movement by some religions to incorporate the deviant into the religious mainstream. Some pastors and parish priests are ministering to congregations composed of homosexuals and prostitutes. This general agreement on the nature of the immoral act has led to an interesting paradox, which is that usually whenever the word "immoral" is used, it carries with it the connotation of sexual "goings on."

As we examine one area of moral behavior--that of sexual morality--we find different positions and outcomes based on the source of the moral imperative. So a humanist argues for a rational, thought out approach which considers the effect sexual relations would have on the interpersonal relationship, on self-respect, trust and so on.[15] A conservative religion would abide in a more absolute position, e.g., "Thou shalt not commit adultery." Also defined as immoral would be seduction, fornication, homosexuality, prostitution, rape, and other sexual practice proscribed by God. As with other systems of morality, there would be differences within the absolute morality position. Some religions are accepting of homosexuality and others reject this as immoral.

Generally acceptable or moral sexual behavior, at least within the Judaeo-Christian tradition, means restrictive codes of sexual conduct--genital heterosexual monogamy. Premarital and extramarital behavior are forbidden. Others take a position based on adult mutual consent. Generally the law supports the restrictive Judeao-Christian position, but often these laws are overlooked suggesting a change in society away from the restrictive position. This notion of sexual immorality is so deeply imbedded in most people (especially Americans) that when someone speaks of the horrors of war, the napalm, murder and butchery, as being "immoral," the first assumption is that that person is some kind of political "leftist" or "radical." The idea that a war, or war in general, can be considered immoral is foreign to the thinking of some Americans, even after the Viet Nam fiasco. For many, "immoral" is reserved for sex. One must note, however, the growing nuclear freeze movement for whom war is immoral--at least nuclear war!

It must be pointed out that this kind of encapsulated thinking is not entirely the fault of organized religions. Attendance at functions which are primarily of a religious nature has fallen in recent years to the extent that the teachings of organized religions are not accurately resented by their followers, some of whom may be hypocritical. In fact, it is probably true that religious bodies, especially the more fundamentalist branches, still list and

---

[15]Lester A. Kirkendall, "Reflections on Sexual Morality," Humanist, Vol. 32, November/December, 1972, pp. 11-13. See also Judith Frankel O'Augelli and Anthony R. O'Augelli, "Moral Reasoning and Premarital Sexual Behavior: Toward Reasoning About Relationships," Journal of Social Issues, Vol. 33, 1977, pp. 46-66.

crusade against a number of "immoral" behaviors, from
sex to theft and traffic violations.

Moral values which are a result of tradition can
serve as guidelines when there are no other clear-cut
rules. Americans speak of a notion of "fair play,"
they don't "take advantage" of others (outside of
business dealings), they "stick up for the underdog."

An example of the latter notion is the
relationship between Viet Nam and the United States
and, more significantly, between Israel and the United
States. Leaving out of the discussion the possible
practical explanations of American involvement with
Israel, the fact remains that Israel retains
overwhelming popular sympathy in America, even from
people who have absolutely no connection with the
Jewish faith. In the press and in the minds of many
Americans, Israel is the small but powerful underdog
completely surrounded by big bully Arab nations. This
support of Israel has probably been undermined somewhat
with the recent Lebanon invasion; however, that
invasion has solidified Israel's position as the
championed underdog for others. Further examples of
Americans' passion for fair play are reported by
visiting foreigners who generally note that they are
treated cordially and kindly.

These, then, are expected ways of behaving in
American society; they are "moral" and "right."
Similarly, there is the implicit expectation of
reciprocity which specifies that people don't hurt
those who help them and that they strive to repay those
to whom they are indebted for acts of kindness.

Use of the word Tradition implies age, and
certainly there is an element of age involved. The
sociological approach, however, suggests that tradition
is largely a function of the form of organization found
in a society. Tönnies viewed societies as ongoing
entities and postulated distinctive attributes
characteristic of generalized stages of development.
It will be rewarding at this point to take a closer
look at what he had to say in the area of morality.

Tönnies conceived of society as being in a
constant state of movement, and he proposed a
dichotomous situation consisting of the state from
which societies begin their movement, or evolution, and
the end state toward which they are continually

moving.[16] The beginning state he termed Gemeinschaft, and the end state he named Gesellschaft. These two terms come into English as the rough equivalents of Community and Society, respectively. While his conceptualization of the two poles of a continuum included all aspects of human social life, from economic activity to family relationships, we will include here only the elements most pertinent to the topic of moral values. A partial list would include the following:

Gemeinschaft	Gesellschaft
Unity	atomization
solicitous paternalism	compulsory exploitation
relative peace	wars, wholesale slaughter
sympathetic relationships among kinsfolk and old acquaintances	strangers and aliens everywhere
home and land-loving peasants	businessmen
permanency of abode	mobility
folk art, music, handicrafts	science

Clearly each society proscribes behavior which is dysfunctional to it. One way of proscribing behavior is to view it as immoral. Under the Gemeinschaft type of society, a farmer who owned his own land would be more than just perturbed if his son or daughter "dropped out" of society. It would be more than just the wasting of one life, it would be the end of a way of life when he died. "Dropping out" of a Gesellschaft arrangement has fewer consequences which are external to the individual.

Continuing with Tönnies, analysis, it is evident that for him, Gemeinschaft represented the youth of a society while Gesellschaft stood for the adulthood. The Gemeinschaft society represents people functioning according to their "natural will." When asked why they

---

[16]Ferdinan Tönnies, Fundamental Concepts of Sociology. New York: American Book Company, 1940.

40

behave in any particular way in any given social thing they may do, they will have more difficulty in answering than a member of a Gesellschaft level society. In the Gesellschaft stage, people function according to their "rational will."

Tønnies felt that all social relationships are created by human will, either to accomplish some other goal or because the relationship is an end in itself. Similarly, he found that the more the actions of man are controlled by love, understanding, custom, religion, folkways, mores, the less people, animals and things are thought of as mere means to ends and the less important the role of such socially sanctioned means as paper money, tricks of the trade, and the businessman's intellectual ability. As societies come to resemble the Gesellschaft type, they lose much of the concern for the individual, which , as we have seen, is so characteristic of the Gemeinschaft stage.

Not only are certain patterns of behavior more typical of one stage of societal evolution than another, moral values and means of enforcing them are also subject to change as societies evolve. In Gemeinschaft (norms of morality), are sanctioned by religion through its beliefs, faith, and creeds. In Gesellschaft, the norms of morality are sanctioned by public opinion, which arises from common interests.

Tønnies defined three great main laws of the Gemeinschaft society: (1) relatives and married couples love each other; (2) between people who love each other, there is understanding; (3) those who love and understand each other remain and dwell together and organize their common life.

The opposite kinds of feelings are present in the Gesellschaft stage:

In order that a thing may be at all of value in the Gesellschaft, it is only necessary that it be possessed by one party to the exclusion of another and be desired by one or another individual of this latter party. Apart from this requirement all its other characteristics are insignificant.

Gesellschaft exchanges absolute morality for expedient morality. Where in Gemeinschaft one must truly be a "moral" person, in Gesellschaft he must only

41

appear to have whatever moral qualities are in demand at the moment.

From the above it is clear that the stage of development of the society, which in part determines the strength and extent of the traditions, will have a significant effect on the moral values which will be found in the society. Indeed, it may be that in view of Tönnies paradigm the "return to the old values" may be an impossibility given the stage of development of American society.

A third basic way in which moral values become part of systems is through interaction with other social systems. As systems interact with each other there is frequently an exchange in individuals as people immigrate and emmigrate. These individuals come into a new system still laden with the moral values of their original system. American history is the story of the arrival, conglomeration and eventual dispersion of successive waves of immigrant groups. In the process, each group made its contribution to the complex whole that is this country. The American language is one of the most obvious examples of the influence of different cultures, containing as it does thousands of foreign words from aficionado to zealot.

As a system works to socialize its immigrants, there can be two-way communication of values. The infusion of Catholicism and the large number of Catholic immigrants has had an impact ranging from "meatless Fridays" in the recent past to definitions of divorce, adultery, and so on.

Even today there are distinctly different regional "flavors" in different parts of the country. It has become an accepted fact that what is commonly accepted in Los Angeles may be regarded as immoral in many other parts of the country.

Notwithstanding the effects on coming into a new social system, some groups are able to retain many of their original moral values over considerable periods of time. Further study perhaps will identify which groups and, more significantly, for what reasons. The Israelites in Egypt changed little over the many decades of their captivity, and in modern societies there are found nationality groups whose members live in the same general part of a city or state and are able to keep alive their traditions through interaction

42

with one another. As their celebrations and holidays and special diets remind them of their ancestry, they are able to retain some of their moral values and resist the wholesale assimilation which is the ever-present possibility of minority groups who lack obvious racial differences. Many examples could be cited of groups of Swedes, Greeks, Italians and other Europeans who more or less remain together in America.

Parenthetically, it can be added that even obvious racial characteristics are no barrier to the onslaught of host moral variables. Blacks complain of "Uncle Toms" who have adopted the "white man's" system and are therefore untrue to their race. Indians have their "Uncle Tomahawks" who are "red on the outside and white on the inside." Both of these are examples of the inconsistency which can result from incomplete assimilation and conflict of roles as people try to find a path between two different systems of moral values.

The final category of sources of moral values can be described as the pragmatic orientation. This label implies that whatever is found to be functional or productive for the system, whatever serves to prolong the life and achieve the goals of the system, is incorporated somehow into the moral values of the system. Conversely, whatever contributes to the destruction of the system or prevents it from achieving its goals is subsequently incorporated into the morality of the system in such a way as to indicate to people that it is not acceptable behavior.

The above is, at first glance, a rather wide-open kind of definition, but when it is applied to a specific system it can be of significant value. We will not argue here about the special interest groups and their particular goals or efforts to maintain or institute a system functional to them. The definition speaks of system goals and of behaviors as being either functional or dysfunctional vis-a-vis those goals. By extension, then, a system with a poorly defined or poorly accepted set of totals and priorities will be a system with a poorly defined system of moral values. Poor definition of goals in a society is not synonymous with "primitive" or "backward." On the contrary, some so-called primitive societies have a sharply defined set of goals and an equally sharply defined set of moral values. A remote tribe of aboriginal pygmies may devote all of their efforts to the daily task of food

43

gathering, and the moral values will clearly state (will be clearly understood) the duties and taboos which are to be observed. In this kind of situation, the violation of a moral principle may result in disaster for the offender and/or his whole community. The society has to gather food each day or it will go hungry. If a man on guard duty falls asleep and fails to sound the alarm at the first sign of danger, for instance the approach of a lion or some other dangerous situation, there is the very real danger that someone will be killed, or at least that the activities of the whole community will be disrupted.

Extending this line of reasoning to modern American society, it is clear that there are some fundamental differences, but equally clear that the argument holds. American society no longer has (assuming that at one point in time it did have) a set of goals to which all (or even a large number of) Americans would subscribe. The temper of American society can be expressed by the following statement: "I've got mine, baby, you get yours." The government is seen as a source of power to keep one segment of the population from completely dominating the others. Applying the second half of the argument to this situation, one would postulate that in its present fragmented condition (with regards to goals), there would be an equally fragmented set of moral values. It seems obvious that this is in fact the case.

Nevertheless, even a fragmented, disunited society develops moral values through the pragmatic process, by advocating or pronouncing as right those things which contribute to the maintenance of the status quo, and by labeling as wrong those things which threaten some segment or practice of the system. For example, some view the legalization of marijuana at this point in time as a pipe dream. They assert that it would be extremely dysfunctional--leaving aside any possible physiological consequences--to several powerful parts of the system. The organized liquor and tobacco industries, to name just two, stand to lose tremendous amounts of money, both in terms of lost sales and diminished demand. It can be safely assumed that if marijuana is ever legalized it will be along guidelines established with the consent of the tobacco and liquor industries.

From the experiences of daily life many things become apparent which are either good or bad for the system. In this way functional activities take on the "right" moral overtones and dysfunctional activities come to be seen as "wrong."

Within this pragmatic context, then, it is clear that Spencer recognized one of the principle source of moral values when he argued that the character of the aggregate represented the character of the units. A reformulation of this idea can be stated: "What the family is, such will society be" (Sorokin, 1927). Spencer concluded from his work in the field of sociology that ". . . no one can be perfectly free till all are free; no one can be perfectly moral till all are moral; no one can be perfectly happy till all are happy" (1971).

Probably there is some overlap in the development of moral values. It is difficult to say, "this value is a result of this kind of activity." The principle forces at work in the area of the development of moral values and how they interrelate is not totally understood at this point.

Once a moral value has become part of a system, what does it mean? Since words have only the meanings that we assign them, there must be some mechanism in society responsible for a standardizing effect. This mechanism is known as socialization. Because the term socialization includes many things, the term "transmission" will be used as a more restricted concept concerning itself with the transmission of moral values. There are two principle approaches concerning the transmission of moral values. One approach states that morality is a part of the personality, that the personality is "formed" at a certain stage of life, or is formed over a period of time and the individual goes through a number of "stages," each accompanied by a number of characteristic behavior patterns and though processes. Not surprising, then, in view of this stage theory, is the fact that much of the moral development literature consists of attempts to construct "types," each of which is characterized by certain traits and/or

45

behaviors.[17] When one takes the psychological approach, there are two principle options open to him. He can conclude that immoral behavior is rooted in something which happened to the individual in his early life, or he can view immoral behavior as evidence of arrested development. Some of Kohlberg's work suggests that a stage concept can be useful, especially since it has enabled him to come up with some ways of helping children progress the to next highest stage. It has long been a goal of many educators to be able to teach their pupils to behave in a moral fashion, and specific tools will be welcomed in this area.

On the other hand, the sociological approach holds that moral values, i.e., morality, are a property of groups rather than individuals. As this notion is elaborated it will become apparent that it encompasses and envisions the work of Kohlberg and others who take the psychological approach.

Every man is a member of a system indeed as the French sociologist Emile Durkheim said: "The only question a man can ask is not whether he can live outside society, but in what society he wishes to live." But before a person can be considered in his position within a system, other factors relating to the person must be considered, for they play a part in the making of the man. These are termed individual factors, and they help to determine why an individual behaves the way he does.

There are perhaps factors of a spiritual nature which are present as overtones, and they are presented for consideration here as real phenomena, which may play a role in the determination of human behavior. Such phenomena, however, are not available to scientific study and may more properly be the topic of a philosophical or religious paper. The fact that they are unverified in a scientific sense does not demonstrate nonexistence.

[17]R. J. Havighurst and H. Taba, Adolescent Character and Personality, New York: John Wiley, 1949; R. H. Peck and R. J. Havigurst, The Psychology of Character Development, New York: John Wiley, 1960; Lawrence Kohlberg, "The Development of Children's Orientations Toward a Moral Order," Vita Humana, Vol. 6, 1-2, 1973.

The biological factor refers to genetic (inherited) as well as acquired physical characteristics. Included in this category would be the intelligence quotient, the physical body with its attendant abilities and limitations, and any inherited assets or liabilities. For example, there may be a genetic factor involved in the occurrence of schizophrenia. While some dismiss the biological factor, certainly it must be accounted for in some sense, at least as a limiting factor. In past times there was a conviction that like father, like son, and that the sons of criminals and "crazy people" would naturally grow up to become the same kinds of criminals and crazy people because of the presence of the genetic factor. While the most recent studies by medical doctors and geneticists indicate that there may be some truth in this assumption, the extent to which it is true is not known. Certainly, however, it is not the most important factor, for studies of one-egg twins have shown that other factors can cause people who are almost biologically identical to exhibit quite different personalities. In the area of moral development, then, it must be kept in mind that the body and the brain remain biological mechanisms, and as such are subject to the influence of a host of variables, from genetic factors to anchovy pizza, any or all of which may be capable of altering behavior.

Since it is not the purpose of this work to engage in physiological reductionism, the next factor which is of primary significance is the social factor. This will be discussed in more detail later on, so at this point it will suffice to state that the social factor is the "environment," the total social and physical milieu, in which the person is immersed.

The attitude factor is defined here as the way one looks at life, and it is safe to assume that it is, like the social factor, largely a product of the system in which the individual is living. The social and attitude factors in combination forge a mental alloy that is particularly resistant to change. For example, there is a tribe of South American Indians which refuses to use fishhooks. They obtain fish by spearing them, and when the water is cloudy at certain times of the year they are unable to eat their regular diet. Even after being shown the great utility of the fishhook, they refuse to experiment with it.

47

Some argue that there is some substance to the legendary notion that each nationality has some clearly identifiable personality characteristics present in its individual members. One of these characteristics is the attitude factor, the way the individual looks at life. Are some peoples just naturally happy, are others reserved, calculating, trusting? Without indulging in popular notions which may be groundless, it is stated that a nationality (or, to be more precise, a social system) is capable of producing more of one attitude type than another. This means that it is very possible for a majority of the members of a given system to possess the characteristics for which their system is noted.

From the above it is clear that regardless of his position in society, a person's behavior will be influenced by the combination of individual factors at work in his life. These factors, then, the spiritual, biological, social and attitude, are present in every individual and will react in certain ways with the external stimuli with which the individual comes into contact as he goes through life. They will filter the incoming messages from the previously discussed sources of moral values, and will be partially responsible for the fact that seldom is there complete and total agreement on or adherence to any given system of morality.

Chapter V

MORAL CHANGE

As stated previously during the discussion of the
sociological approach to the problem of moral
development, morality is a property of groups.
Accepting this, how does one account for moral change
(changes in morality)? How does one explain a person
adopting a new moral code and abandoning the old one
under which he had been living and perhaps been raised?

Examples of this change abound today. Certainly
the Watergate affair and its subsequent disclosures of
wrongdoing at the highest levels of power in America is
an example. It appears that a large number of people
who should have "known better" abruptly began behaving
as if the system under which they had been raised, and
which they were supposed to be representing no longer
had any meaning for them.

While it may be easy for participants and
onlookers to the Watergate affair to rationalize the
behavior that took place, rationalization may not be
useful to adequately cope with some of the other events
in modern America (and, by extension, other modern
nations). It raises an even thornier problem when
these kinds of situations can be reproduced in the
laboratory using human subjects. Some examples of both
kinds of situations, laboratory and "natural," follow.

This first example is of a rare situation, rare
mainly because of the fact that true experimental
situations using human beings, situations in which the
experimenter controls the entire situation, are rare in
the social sciences for numerous reasons. The results
of this experiment may (unhappily) be used by the
non-scientist as justification for the prevention of
future laboratory experiments.

The laboratory was located on the campus of
Stanford University. In the basement of one of the
buildings the experimenters partitioned off an area and
remodeled it extensively. At the end of the remodeling
they had an exact replica of a jail. There were barred
cells with locks on the doors, dingy walls and
ceilings, and no identifiable access to the outside
world. Bare lightbulbs revealed the drab realness of

49

the laboratory as final preparations were made to receive the subjects of the experiment.

The subjects were carefully chosen to eliminate any potential trouble from psychological upset at the conditions they would be undergoing. Tests were given and carefully checked to ensure that the subjects chosen were among the most healthy, well-adjusted students on the campus. One of the basic purposes of the experiment was to determine the effects of a new and different environment on the personalities of well-educated, intelligent and well-adjusted young college-age men.

The sample of men finally selected was divided into two groups, one designated the "jailers" and the other "prisoners." The experiment was designed to run for 14 days during which time the experimenters would observe the different ways in which the subjects reacted to the experimental stimulus of either being in a jail as prisoners or being in charge of prisoners as guards. In addition to the carefully constructed "jail," there were such other facsimiles of a real jail as uniforms, jail-type bunks, etc. The actual experiment began when the experimenters sent the police around to the homes of the subjects who had been placed in the prisoner group and had the prisoners all arrested and taken away to being in a jail in a police car. In an effort to increase the depersonalizing effects of the jail, the experimenters had the prisoners wear a dress-like garment. The toilet facilities were not in the cells, so that in order to use any sanitary facilities a prisoner had to ask a guard to be taken out and the whole procedure was done under the eyes of the guards. The setting of the experiment was so effective that the experiment had to be called off after six days, because of the effects which were being observed in the subjects. Some of the prisoners had begun to behave in some extreme ways, which included crying fits, depression, and so on, as a result of the way they had been treated by the jailers.

What had happened was that these normal college boys (nice boys, one could say) had completely taken on the roles of the people they were pretending to be. The guards became prison guards in the full sense of the term, exhibiting overall the whole spectrum of behaviors which are usually associated with prison guards. This taking of the guard role referred to their behavior with regards to the whole experiment,

50

not just to the way they treated the prisoners. The guards became guards to each other and interacted with each other as if they were all in fact guards. Some of the guards engaged in sadistic and brutal treatment of the prisoners, taunting and tormenting them. This is a shocking enough thing by itself, but it is equally distressing that none of the other guards interfered with the mean ones. They all had become guards and had taken the role almost completely, even to the observing of the "unwritten rules" like not interfering.

Similarly, the prisoners had undergone a transformation. contrary to the romantic notion of intelligent men remaining intelligent men under all conditions, the prisoners became totally immersed in their prison situation and talked about little outside of the prison context. Lofty ideals were forgotten in the daily struggle with the guards. The whole situation is compounded by the fact that none of the subjects were given any kind of specific instructions with regards to the way they should behave or how they should treat each other. The resulting behavior was a result of their own interpretation of the way a guard or prisoner should react.

From the results of the pre-experimental screening tests, the actual results of the experiments are disconcerting to say the least. What is the explanation for the way those normal, adequately socialized young men declined so far in so short a period of time?

A second example of a situation in which people behave in a way far different from what is expected of them is found in a recent study[18] done by a high school teacher dealing with the honesty of his students. The high school where the man teaches is located in an area where there is great emphasis on religious values and some of the pupils involved in the experiment come from homes where the fathers are members of the leading councils of local churches. By implication, then, it was expected that the prevalence of a religious atmosphere would predispose the students to act in honest (moral) ways. The teacher administered a true/false examination to the class, and then gathered up the exams and (without the knowledge of the

---

[18]Unpublished study in possession of author.

students) took them to be photocopied. The next day he returned the original papers to the students and told them that they were going to grade their own papers. As far as any of them knew, it was not a part of any experiment, but only another test. Taking the graded papers, he compared them with the photocopies of the original papers, and found that 80 percent of the students in his class had changed some of the answers on their examinations.

A third example took place at a large university which requires all students to sign an "honor code" document and then expects honest behavior from its students. For several years the university had a program whereby students could earn one-half a semester hour by simply attending weekly assemblies where lectures and forums were presented. The assemblies were held in a large assembly auditorium and the general public was invited from the surrounding community and attendance at the lectures was not recorded. The university expected that its students would honestly attend the minimum number of assemblies required to get the half-hour of credit. The procedure was that at the end of each semester, the students would come to the last scheduled assembly and fill out a form indicating which assemblies they had attended during the semester. If they indicated that they had not attended the minimum required, they would not receive the credit. As a check on the adequacy of the system, the assemblies were monitored for a semester and an actual head count was taken to indicate exactly how many people had attended each assembly. At the end of the semester the results of both the head counts and the reported attendance from the students were compared. The results indicated that the honor code was not being taken seriously by a large number of students. At one assembly where by actual count there had been fewer that 3,000 people in attendance including the general public, over 8,000 students claimed that they had been there.

A fourth example deals with a study done in an area where the dominant religion in the area was attempting to discourage its members from shopping on Sunday as part of a general orientation toward keeping the "Sabbath day" holy. The study interviewed people who shopped on Sunday and came to the conclusion that there are no Sunday shoppers. People who did shop on Sunday defined what they were doing as something different from shopping and did not consider themselves

to be Sunday shoppers.[19] This is a more clear-cut
example of what may have been taking place in the
previous examples. People may define their activities
as being right or moral and then proceed with them even
though they may be in literal violation of established
customs or legal statutes. This may be the process at
work in the widespread violation of the 55 mph speed
limit. People simply define their situation as taking
precedence over the law. Certainly there must be some
explanation for the differential obedience to laws that
is found in almost all societies.

The incident at My Lai, during the Viet Nam war,
is one for which Americans should be seeking an
explanation. Almost every kind of moral value that is
held sacred to Americans was violated in My Lai on the
day of the massacre by a crosssection of American young
men. This was a case of the Stanford jail experiment
run wild. There are many theories which attempt to
explain what happened, and in the final analysis it may
be up to the actual participants to write the final
chapter. The example of My Lai says that men can be
expected to do whatever the system and the circumstance
seem to require, without reference to any kind of
absolute authority or higher, overriding concern.
Milgram's obedience to authority findings do not
support the notion of a generalized lack of individaul
morality, however.

Historically, it has been the case that one system
has been able to take over another system and life goes
on in much the same fashion. Soldiers take up the
sword for the army of their conqueror, politicians
administer the legal systems of invaders, and the
police are invariably on the side of whoever is calling
the tune.

Clearly, then, there are situations every day in
which we see people behaving contrary to the commonly
accepted morality of their system. It sidesteps the
question to merely dismiss all these people as deviant.

As has been stated above, morality is a property
of groups rather than individuals. Let us arrive at

---

[19]Franklyn W. Dunford and Phillip R. Kunz, "The
Neutralization of Religious Dissonance," Review of
Religious Research, Vol. 15, 1973, pp. 1-8.

working definitions of the terms "groups" and "society" and "system" before using them in the following discussion. It has recently become fashionable to speak of "sub-culture" or "sub system" in dealing with deviant groups, e.g., "hippies." This implies that only the majority group--the dominant system--can be considered a full-fledged system--that other systems are somehow incomplete. Aberle and his associates write convincingly about the functional requisites of a society, and his guidelines are no doubt valid in certain contexts. In contrast to this point of view, however, it is proposed that there are few, if any, subsystems; that rather there are systems large and small, close and separate (for purposes of this work, group and society and system are used interchangeably without a great deal of elaboration of the finer shades of difference implied in each term). Granted there are qualitative and quantitative differences between systems, but to see a system as merely some kind of offshoot, as something less than a complete system, is to begin an investigation with a false position. Certainly there will be numerous similarities between two systems with the same basic culture, i.e., common language, etc. (although it is common for a system to develop its own cant, usually two people from different systems will be able to communicate by resorting to the mother tongue), but that must not be allowed to obscure the fact that there are also unique differences.

System Selection

        Consequently, we hold that within any given culture there may be a multiplicity of systems. What, then, induces one man to become a member of a different system? We see one significant element involved in a system selection as being the individual factors mentioned earlier. It is not proposed, however, that by themselves they can account for anywhere near the total variance. Additionally, it is necessary to see at the outset that the social and attitude factors are almost wholly a function of the systems into which a person is accepted as a member, either by birth or immigration. Hence we are concerned with indicators like social class, occupation and education, rather than with variables of a more restricted, psychological nature (e.g., age at which an individual was toilet trained).

Of course individuals within a society can adhere to smaller systems, from which they derive their values, and develop a personal code stronger and more appropriate to his or her needs than that promulgated by the larger society.

Shakespeare said that the world is a stage and the people in it are merely players. In a manner of speaking, he was right. We have already seen that there can be many systems within a given culture. We can compare each of these systems to an army. An army is more than just a mass of individuals, since there is an established order, and most important, like Shakespeare said, there are a number of roles. In an army the roles are divided into ranks and areas of responsibility. Corresponding to the ranks and positions in an army, societies have positions and roles.

Positions and Roles

A position is a place in society with its attendant rights and responsibilities. A role is the dynamic aspect of a position; it is the carrying out of the rights and responsibilities. What we saw in the Stanford jail experiment as described above was a case of people taking on new roles. A role in a system--like its theatrical counterpart--includes everything a person needs to perform it, generally speaking. There is usually a notion of ranking on some hierarchical scale so that a person knows who is above and below him as well as who is approximately equal. In addition, there are general guidelines regarding behavior and attitudes. This doesn't say that every person who is involved in playing a role will do everything the way he is supposed to, but it does say that if he should not fulfill the expectations of the role model he will experience some conflict. This conflict can come in the form of sanctions from other people or a number of other ways. Just as theatergoers saw Marlon Brando perform as "Zapata," the experimenters in the Stanford jail experiment saw Stanford students perform as prisoners and guards. The Stanford students "became" (temporarily) the roles they had been assigned.

We are proposing that this is indeed what happens. Rather than an individual being "himself" and having society conform to him, society provides a number of roles for each individual, with expectations that the individual behave in a particular prescribed manner while playing a particular role. A man may be a husband, father, employee, member of a religion, etc., simultaneously. Each of these roles may make different--and at times conflicting--demands on him. When a man is fulfilling the obligations of one role, he may at the same time be behaving in an "immoral" manner when measured against the requirements of one of his other roles. It is problematic whether there are moral positions extending across all of one's roles or whether each role may have a different set of moral expectations. We now turn to an examination of some of the cases mentioned earlier in the light of what we have said about the concept of roles, positions, systems, etc.

The Stanford jail experiment was a clear case of a group of people coming into contact with a new and different set of roles and then rapidly adopting the new set. The implication of the experiment is that people are socialized to follow roles, or to play roles. This means that as a child grows he moves into and out of stages (to borrow from the developmental psychology literature) which in reality are role sets or role clusters. Different things are expected at each level and each level carries differential rewards and punishments for a variety of behaviors. The child is taught to recognize and adhere to whatever role-related rules and regulations apply to him by virtue of the roles he is currently playing. Children raised (socialized) in such a manner will not be subject to the modifying power of moral absolutes such as the ten commandments of the Old Testament because of the conflict involved in the carrying out of the roles. The moral "conscience," then, becomes a combination of the behaviors prohibited and allowed by the role set and the internal influence which may make an individual uncomfortable to varying degrees when he engages in certain behaviors. The source of this kind of discomfort may be due to either the individual factors or some residue from earlier roles and teachings.

The high school students who cheated on the exam must have perceived their roles as students as being more important than their roles as children (family name-bearers) of fathers or their roles as religious people. The role of student demands good grades and places emphasis on the end to the exclusion of regulating the means. The students saw an opportunity

56

for a cheap grade by just changing a few answers and they went for it. Receiving the good grade was a fulfillment of the student role, and the desire to fulfill that role must have been sufficiently strong to overpower the honesty and integrity requirements of other roles.

Similarly, the university cheating experience, where the students obtained college credit by telling a small lie indicates that at times one role can dominate the attention, if not the sensibilities, of an individual. This notion, though it may be repellant to the moral person, is a functional one. When a person goes out for a job, the employer is interested in the transcript and is not likely to ask point blank if the candidate ever cheated in school. Even if he were to ask such a question, it is safe to assume that the students, like the Sunday shoppers, would reply with a genuinely heartfelt "no," indicating that they had rationalized their behavior to reduce conflict among their several roles.

As in the case of the jail experiment, the Viet Nam (My Lai) incident involved men taking on the new role of soldier, and playing it--like the college jailers--to the hilt. Again the implication is that those involved had been socialized to become role players more than to be rational human beings who weigh and consider the consequences of their actions. The system in which the roles are found also exerts some influence on the actors and also helps to determine the rightness and wrongness of roles. An example is the fact that Americans who renounce their citizenship and live in a Communist country are seen as traitors, while people who risk their lives to get over the Berlin wall are hailed as "brave defectors."

From the above it is clear that roles, positions, and systems all play important parts in the determination of what is and what is not moral and that they work together on the individual as he is being socialized to insure that he will become a willing actor, and a reliable actor. Few things are more disruptive to a social system than unpredictability. Systems must be able to predict in an accurate manner the approximate behavior which can be expected in a given situation.

As one contemplates various facets of morality and how to assess the moral position of the constituency of society, there are several problems which soon become rather perplexing. Thus we find that those norms which come to represent moral positions still retain some flexibility and are formed in a particular context. Let us consider for a moment the problem of the informant. We ask the question, when is it appropriate to inform? Let us take for the moment the case of informing on one's employer. We have a rather strongly verbalized norm which has even been converted to verse which indicates that "When you work for a man, be loyal to him as long as you work for him." Now the question is, can you inform on your employer and still exhibit loyalty? Obviously this depends in part upon the position you occupy relative to the informing. If, for example, you are the employer, then the norm that says employees ought to be loyal and under no circumstances ought to inform would be most valid. If, on the other hand, you are the informer, or the potential informer, you are not very comfortable with that position realizing that there ought to be a certain amount of loyalty attached to the employer. On the other hand, the circumstances may require telling someone outside the system.

Thus, again referring to Watergate, those who are employed by the Presidency ought to be loyal to the Presidency and supportive of its position. On the other hand, as a third kind of member, that is, as citizens not involved in Watergate, one may ask in righteous indignation, why those men who were involved did not inform, why did they not tell someone what they were required to do? The question is asked in such a manner as to doubt that informing didn't occur to them and that there should have been no question but what they would inform.

In the end, of course, "Deep Throat" did inform to Woodward and Bernstein and thus blew the whole cover-up out of the water. Sometimes informing does occur although the system is not very supportive of informers. Some local jurisdictions are not passing regulations to give informers some amount of protection, however.

So we see that deciding when to inform or not to inform in and of itself becomes a major kind of focal point in terms of consideration of morality. We observe that recent informers have not fared well either in the organization they were informing on or the one they were telling to. As indicated in another place, the informer from another country, that is a citizen of another country who turns traitor or decides to defect or give up his citizenship may indeed inform on the other country and be treated with a great deal of enthusiastic reception on the part of the country to which he defects. He becomes a kind of hero. On the other hand, those citizens of our own country who decide to inform relative to our own country and give secrets to another country are seen as spies, traitors, and villains, and may be treated with contempt and death. Whether or not informing is good, as one considers the Revolutionary War in the United States, depends on whether you are a British subject or a citizen in one of the colonies.

In addition, the particular role one plays in a society also relates to whether or not he might logically serve as an informer. For example, a lawyer who represents a client would be violating his legal ethics and the professional conduct of attorneys if he were to inform against his client. Indeed he may be disbarred for doing so. He is required on the other hand to protect the interest of his client. Thus he may withhold evidence, as may the prosecutor, and indeed this is oftentimes done and rather fully supported by the legal system, although people not understanding the legal system may emit a great deal of criticism for such behavior if it becomes public knowledge.

In some roles there is a type of relationship which has been respected by the courts as privileged information. Thus the information given by a parishioner to a priest or by the client to the attorney is generally so regarded. Other areas are somewhat nebulous and not very well defined in the court system, but are moving toward that kind of position. Thus, currently at least, informers to the news media are sometimes protected by the news media which want to maintain a good relationship with the source, but the courts do not always view this as privileged communication and indeed the journalist may have to suffer the consequences of not fitting in the category which would be defined as privileged information. People passing judgment on the journalist in such a situation may rationalize that he has low morals, that he does not place the values in the right position, that there are things in society which are more important than the trust relationship which the journalist has promised to this source.

59

Clearly, then, the concept of role is a significant element of the question of moral development. "Development" is another word which bears defining. Usually there is a connotation of "improvement" when the word development is used, but this is not necessarily the case. In the discussion of moral development, no implication of goodness is intended, although from an altruistic standpoint it would probably be a good thing if people were constantly involved in improving their morals. What the term implies, then, is change, since, as we have seen, people are capable of making rather rapid and drastic changes in their moral positions.

Consequently, it appears important in making moral judgments to decide whether an act or an individual is being judged. It is certainly acceptable to say that according to the values which are part of one's role set and system, act "X" is an immoral act. But before accusing a person of being an immoral individual one must have an understanding of the context of the situation. Clearly, then, the notion of a system of moral absolutes must be explained in great detail before it can be subscribed to by a logical individual. There may be a system of absolutes, which is to say that God may have certain guidelines for human behavior. But people who are ignorant of those guidelines, or who live in a system which rejects them, cannot logically be held accountable for guideline-violating behavior at this point in their existence. Even within systems there are seldom any absolute moral values. With the possible exception of incest, there are situations in which the moral values of a society may be violated and the violator will be justified, e.g., justifiable homicide occurs from time to time in this country. Incest and other sex-related offenses are more difficult (if not impossible) to justify, although people get involved in deviant systems which emphasize practices which are anathema to the regular system.

When faced with any situation, there are a number of alternatives from which an individual can select a course of action. When he is considering which course to follow, his decision is guided by the fact that whatever he chooses to do, it must be consistent with his role. This is the first set of limitations. From the range of alternatives compatible with the role, he must then select a course of action compatible with his individual factors. These individual factors are the

60

second set of limitations. To illustrate this concept, we present the following hypothetical case of an individual involved in a Watergate-type affair.

Actor J occupies a position as an assistant to the President of the United States. His role, then, is the carrying out of the responsibilities and duties associated with the position. When he is at the office or otherwise functioning in an official capacity, he sees himself as J, assistant to the President of the United States. He may be conscious of the other roles he is responsible for, such as father, husband, lawyer, etc., but his chief concern will be with the prestigious job he has as assistant. The hypothetical situation could be as follows: the President asks J to do something which is clearly illegal. The range of all possible alternatives open to J at the moment as a human being include everything from striking the President to blackmailing him on the spot. However, the role of assistant permits a much more restricted range, say from quitting his post as assistant to accepting the illegal assignment on the spot. Before J makes a decision, the facts are filtered through his individual factors, which may or may not further limit the range of acceptable alternatives. He may at this point experience role conflict, especially if he happens to consider the proposal in the light of some of his other roles which carry obvious restrictions prohibiting the illegal kind of thing he is considering doing. Admittedly the above example is simplified, but it is an illustration of some of the processes involved in making a decision. In reality we cannot expect to find that most people behave as "role-robots," functioning blindly in the role they are playing at the moment without considering their other roles. Rather, it is likely that behavior is a matter of the weighing and trading off of the demands of the different roles an individual plays. As Hindelang (1972) found, people engaging in illegal activities come to develop a value system which condones or at least permits such activity. This finding is consistent with what we have said to this point and inconsistent with a body of literature in the area of criminology which suggests that those engaging in illegal activity hold a value system similar to that of the larger population, and that they have the same knowledge and agreement of what is right and wrong (e.g., Matza and Sykes, 1957). It should not be inferred from the above, however, that the process of selecting behavior from among the choices allowed by the roles in any way makes men more rational. On the contrary, people get locked into certain patterns of behavior to the extent that making a new decision is an almost unheard of occurrence, when it comes to areas laden with moral values. The argument may be made that moral principles are internalized, and that therefore no further external reinforcement is necessary. However, external reinforcement or monitoring may be evident to the individual as a supernatural force (real or imagined) or even as the "generalized other."

A famous American sociologist, W. I. Thomas, taught that whatever people define as real is real in its consequences.[20] This means that before attempting to analyze a situation, one must first arrive at an explanation of the way the situation has been interpreted by the actors involved. Before one can understand why a person behaves the way he does, one must understand what he is thinking at the time, insofar as that is possible. An example of this would be the old custom once found among certain Eskimo tribes wherein the man of the house (igloo) shares his wife with his visiting neighbors. If an Eskimo shares his wife with another Eskimo, and that is an accepted practice in his society, then he has not been immoral in his own eyes or in the eyes of his peers. By contrast, wife-sharing is still considered an immoral type of behavior for most in the American society. Even "swingers" may feel their behavior to be wrong by general standards.

Clearly, then, in understanding and explaining human moral development and human behavior, not only must one have some understanding of what a person is thinking, he must also have an overview of the entire context of the situation. One of the characteristics of organized religions is the fact that they tend to brand as immoral that which is merely different. There is widespread ignorance of the fact that morality, since it is a property of groups, may therefore differ from group to group. Returning to the example of marriage, plural marriage is not only considered immoral in America, it is punishable by law (although this may change in the near future), while in the

---

[20]William I. Thomas and Dorothy Swaine Thomas, The Child in America, New York: Knopf, 1928, p. 572.

Middle East and in certain other areas and cultures, plural marriage is an accepted part of the social system.

We see, then, that societies are able to establish and transmit to their new members certain moral values. Societies also have the ability to enforce their rules, through the mechanism of sanctions. A sanction is anything that A does to B to get him to behave the way A wants him to. We can identify six basic aspects of sanction: positive, negative, formal, informal, external, internal.

External sanctions are those which are placed on an individual by others. Internal sanctions, on the other hand, are not visible and they affect a person from within. An example of an internal sanction would be the feeling a person gets from behaving a certain way: a positive feeling in the case of the joy felt after saving someone's life, or a negative feeling, like the shame and embarrassment that causes some people to walk backward into X-rated movies.

Formal sanctions are official ways of controlling behavior, e.g., prison (a negative formal sanction), or a medal (a positive formal sanction). Informal sanctions may be official but they are not concrete like formal sanctions. An example of a positive informal external sanction would be respect. In dealing with formal and informal we have alluded to the positive and negative sanctions as well. Prisons and medals are, respectively, negative and positive external formal sanctions. All "offenders" (people who violate the moral values of a society) are not dealt with in the same way.

Americans have seen that their former Vice president has not been imprisoned where a less-famous individual convicted of the same crime would perhaps be spending time behind bars. The Vice president was dealt however, with the negative, formal, external sanction of disbarment.

From the above it is clear that societies, through various means, are able to play a significant role in the development of individual behavior patterns. We now return to an examination of the relationship between societies and the transmission of moral values.

Transmission

Ideally, as each child is raised and each immigrant is indoctrinated, the whole system of moral values that a society holds should be passed on, i.e., transmitted intact, to the newcomers. If transmission were in fact carried out in this fashion, there would be little abrupt change in a society, because everyone would be alike. Surely this is neither possible nor desirable.

In reality, then, transmission is accomplished through the interaction of several forces. At the outset we state that the family is one of the most significant single elements involved in the process of moral development. There are several reasons for this. First, it may be possible for the family to instill a particular set of moral standards in a child so deeply that he will identify with those standards his whole life to the exclusion of all others. This could be a profitable situation or a disastrous one. A child raised by a family of professional thieves may have an excellent chance of becoming a professional thief, especially if his parents raise him to that end. Conversely, a child raised by moral people may have a good chance of becoming a moral person himself. The idea of socialization may inculcate in the child a proclivity to seek out and associate with only those people whose standards are similar to his own. It seems that a look at either end of the spectrum will serve to reinforce this point of view. There are religious groups which pass on from generation to generation the same set of principles (e.g., Jews, Hindus) and there is little intergenerational variance. At the other end of the spectrum are families who from generation to generation are in trouble with the law, are on welfare, are chronically underemployed and undereducated. These latter families and groups do not represent the failure of a system as much as they represent the presence of two distinct systems.

Secondly, as a result of being raised in a particular kind of family, the child may find that he can meet all of his needs in ways approved of by his family, without having to go outside his system. In some cases he may not even have the opportunity to go outside his restricted system, as in the case of many rural areas and of some highly urbanized areas as well. The more interchange there is between systems, the greater is the probability of change.

A principle element in transmission and in moral development is the concept of internalization. Internalization may be defined as an individual learning to follow the rules of society even though he wants to transgress and where no one is watching and therefore able to punish. Basically, we can see internalization as a kind of "conscience." What Kohlberg was talking about was what a person will do when he is sure he will never be found out. Here again we go back to the forces at work in systems. If a person behaves a certain way because of fear of detection and punishment (either by the law or by some supernatural source of power), then he is responding to internal or external sanction. Using our definition of sanctions, then, we see internalized behavior as that behavior which a person decides to follow when there is no possibility of external sanctions being applied and there are no internal sanctions which serve as instruments of force. When dealing with the question of internalization, it is necessary to seek empirical data, since experiments indicate that what a person says he will do is not necessarily what he will in fact do. Internalization is generally defined as the process of an individual acquiring a norm to the extent that it becomes part of him and no longer needs external reinforcement in order to keep it viable. The problem is that one may assume internalization and in the absence of negative behavior would believe that the internalization was complete. On the other hand, if there is negative behavior, then one simply redefines and says obviously he hadn't internalized the norm. The concept creates problems in that an individual who is behaving appropriately, that is, staying withing the normative behavior, may be doing so not because he has internalized the norm, but because there is indeed external reinforcement or external observation on the part of the "generalized other" about which Cooley and Mead talk or on the part of supernatural beings, even, whom he believes to be monitoring his activity and which will require accounting for that activity at some future point.

Chapter VI

LEVELS OF MORALITY

Even though a family or a system does its best to indoctrinate new members, there are differing degrees of acceptance of the system values. Angell[21] describes three levels of morality which illustrate this point. Genuine adherence, the first level, describes a condition similar to internalization. The genuine adherent obeys the rules of his system without questioning or calculating. He has internalized the values and he needs no supervision in his behavior. It is this kind of person to which Riesman referred in his description of "inner-directed" types.[22] Expedient adherence, the second of Angell's levels, involves a calculation of the consequences associated with a particular behavior. Any rational person can see that the possible consequences far outweigh any possible advantage to be found in overt criminal activity, such as the armed robbery of a bank. But a clever accountant may carefully plan, figure and weigh all possible outcomes in deciding whether or not to embezzle funds from his employers. He may even calculate the amount he could steal and compare it with the possible prison term, and if it came out to an acceptable dollar per year figure, he might then go ahead and steal. Indeed, if he did not posit any "afterlife tally sheet" such behavior might even be rational from his point of view. Several experiments have shown that expedient adherence is the most common type. Speed limits in particular and traffic laws in general are widely regarded as things to be observed only when in the presence of a policeman. Deviance is the final category under Angell's paradigm of adherence, and it is divided into two sub-types. Deviance may be practiced for its own sake, i.e., for the rewards the specific type of behavior will bring, or it may be that the deviant behavior is a result of an orientation to another system, which means that if A

---

[21]Robert Cooley Angell, Free Society and Moral Crisis, Ann Arbor: The University of Michigan Press, 1938.

[22]David Riesman, The Lonely Crowd, New York: Doubleday and Company, 1953.

is recognized as being a member of system X but deep inside he feels himself a member of system Y, he will be seen as deviant by the members of system X. The Mormons, when they began practicing plural marriage (polygyny), became quite deviant in the eyes of the rest of American society, even though they maintained that they were simply following their new system of orientation.

It seems appropriate here to introduce several additional concepts which will help clarify the subject of moral development. We define "more" as a traditional way of behaving adhered to by the majority of the group which involves a sense of right or wrong. Some examples of modern American mores include definitions of conduct in the areas of pre-marital sexual conduct, interaction with other people and relationship to law.

Generally we think of individual persons as being immoral. We do not question the morality of organizations and institutions to the same extent.

It is possible for individuals within an organization to cause the organization to do things immoral by his own decision. Or, on the other hand, the immorality may exist as part of the structure of the organization.

In the first case a food store owner may instruct his checkers to do something not legal and immoral. In one such case the store owner leaned a broom against the check-out counter and placed a can of floor wax on the counter next to the cash register. He instructed the cashier to charge each customer for the two items along with the other items they had selected. If the customer did not protest the store received the price of the items, and left them there for the next customer. If the customer did protest, the cashier apologized and deducted the amount charged, indicating that he thought the items belonged to the customer also. The items could be "sold" as many as fifty times a day and still stand there to be sold again. This is clearly immoral behavior on the part of the store owner and also the employee.

In the second case the blame is not as easily fixed but still has the same consequences for the customer. The store advertizes various items on sale in the local paper. The items are not repriced, however, and the cashier charges the regular--not on sale--price. Perhaps one could not expect the cashier to memorize all of the sale prices. Perhaps the customer should tell the cashier which items are on sale. To protest to the store owner brings a response that he will talk to the cashier. In such a case most customers pay the regular price while believing that they get the sale price. No one appears to really be to blame. The mechanism of "sales" and "pricing" are stacked against the customer.

In another case a company does not have the funds to raise the salary of certain top-level employees so it instructs them to submit a few extra travel vouchers to increase their income. Thus, the rules of the organization are broken and the employees must resort to dishonesty to receive the pay.

Individuals sometimes place themselves in a position where they have a conflict of interest, that is, a situation where they have personal or corporate interests which are in conflict with other interests they hold--usually of a corporate or public interest. At times such an interest may result from a self-imposed conflict in which the person is attempting, and often achieving, benefits from both sides of the interest, or benefiting personally at the expense of public or corporate trust. On the other hand, the person may find himself in the conflict situation without really being aware how he got there. The moral question then is whether or not he will extirpate himself from the situation, or continue to benefit from the situation. Once a decision is made to maintain the benefiting conflict there is usually a resultant procedure of rationalization as a mechanism of dissonance reduction.

Thus a member of Congress may serve an important position on a key committee for some industry. The Congressman may then accept speaking engagements within that industry, for which there is a handsome honorarium paid--one far more than such a speech could normally command. One must wrestle with the question whether this is influence peddling or providing an informative speech to an interested body who are disinterested in purchasing the influence.

By way of explaining why people behave the way they do, we offer the following definitions of moral action and prudent action. Moral action is action

69

based on others' needs while prudent action is action geared to self-interest. Here again we find that overlap and combination are facts of life. Most action that involves any rational consideration at all can include both moral and prudent considerations. For example, the decision to obey the speed limit in a school zone may involve both fear of a radar trap (prudent consideration) and anxiety over running over a child (moral consideration) and being thrown into jail on a manslaughter charge (prudent consideration).

Clearly, then, it can be seen that individual behavior is a combination of choices, within the context of a role or roles and the rules of a system, involving internalized norms, prudent action and moral action. Human behavior in general is a result of the interrelation of society, roles, and individual factors, which in turn are largely determined by the society.

Chapter VII

SUMMARY

We have discussed the phenomenon of moral development, and stated that rather than "improvement," we interpret development to mean change from one form to another. Changes in moral values, then, are less a result of any specific kinds of internal changes than they are the result of the movement into and out of a continuous succession of roles. As children grow up in a system, they are presented a range of alternatives from which to choose their behavior. It is highly unlikely that a person will behave in a way not offered by his society, which is attested to by the fact that even insane behavior conforms to pre-existing patterns. It is significant that things which are labeled deviant are things which are done in a manner opposite to the normally expected manner.

There are several important elements involved in the socialization process, i.e., the process of learning moral values. Of primary significance is the concept of roles. Each system has within it a number of roles which must be filled. It is possible for one person to play several roles at the same time, that is, it is possible to be involved in several simultaneously even though at any given moment there are usually only a restricted number making demands upon the behavior of the actor. Different roles in a person's repertoire of roles may be attached to different systems, which can be a source of role conflict. When the demands of one role are contrary to the demands of another the stage is set for role conflict and the situation can only be resolved by some kind of action on the part of the actor, whether this action consists of rationalization or complete withdrawal from one of the positions he occupies.

This is consistent with the view that criminals come to develop their own system of morality. If they try to engage in criminal activity and at the same time maintain membership in the straight society, there will be conflict. The conflict can be resolved by either withdrawing from criminal activity or from the straight society. The Watergate affair can serve as an example of this kind of conflict. Men who have roles as lawyers experienced conflict when their roles as government officials demanded illegal behavior which

71

violated their lawyer roles. Whichever role is perceived at the time as being supreme is the role which will prevail with its attendant morality.

A religious educator, in an effort to impart some sense of the value of a personal code of ethics, once made the following analogy: He described a situation in which a person had drawn a circle on the sidewalk. He said that if he then were to give his word that he would not move from the circle, he would in fact not move from it but remain there until released from his pledge. Carrying his analogy one more step, let us suppose that somehow his little child is there and is injured and is bleeding to death. There is no one else there to see him if he decides to step out of the circle. Will he move to save his child or will he let her die so that he can maintain some kind of internal "record." If he moves to save his child, Kohlberg would say that he has reached the highest "stage" of moral development, where human life is more important than laws or other types of systemic restraints. The sociological approach would indicate that if he saves her and leaves the circle he has perceived his role as father or adult as being more important than the role of rigidly upright religious person. If he remains in the circle we would ascribe to him, not morality, but error of judgment.

From this it can be seen that morality is largely determined by the situation. For example, the recent experiences of the survivors of the plane crash on the Chilean mountainside suggest the applicability of this line of reasoning. Normally there is a tremendous taboo on cannibalism, but those men who ate their dead companions are not subject to any sanctions because of the situation under which they committed cannibalistic acts.

Clearly, then, there must be a better way to socialize individuals. At the present time they are socialized to behave as components of systems, and to a large extent their moral values are a function of the system of which they are currently members. This would be an acceptable method if all systems were functional, or moral. Since they aren't there is the continuous battle between systems and a never-ending flow of recruits into all varieties of systems. A better way is needed, in which the decision rule for behavior will be based along the lines of the Christian "golden rule." This is not an empty plea for a return to the "old-time religion," but rather a suggestion that there is a sound sociological basis to the notion that there will be beneficial results to a system in which each member behaves as he would like other members to behave toward him. The implications are staggering and need not be elaborated here beyond the point of saying that a great number of social problems would be solved and life would be better for all system members. What is needed, then, is research into the development and application of ways of changing socialization and behavior patterns to conform to this new goal. "Religion" per se need not even be a part of the program.

Certainly all problems will not be solved and there will still be deviants of both a sociological nature and a psychological nature. The logical place for such research and implementation to begin is the family because of its central role in the socialization of new societal members.

Parenthetically, some immoral behavior is the result of family definitions of the situation. The famous case in New York where 39 people watched as a woman was stabbed to death may have been such a case. Anyone familiar with the nature of family fights and police work knows that a policeman is most likely to be killed when he intervenes in a family fight. In these cases the two (or more) combatants frequently turn unitedly on anyone who attempts to break up the fight. By extension, then, the 39 people may have defined the situation as a family fight and decided on that basis not to get involved. Other situations of this type yield information which suggests that people refrain from intervention not because they are unconcerned or immoral, but because the situation is somewhat ambiguous.

In conclusion it seems apparent that individuals are taught from birth to heed the rules of the roles they are playing and the systems within which those roles are acted out. The problem does not seem to lie in the transmission process as a process, but rather with the content of the process. It seems that a better system would result if people were taught several principles within the boundaries of which they could make all their decisions. This is not a call for moral absolutes, but is a suggestion that the socialization process should teach its newcomers to behave as rational, thinking beings, along the lines of

Kohlberg's sixth stage. At the present time the development of moral values in people is left to chance in a large number of cases as people are taught rules and not principles.

REFERENCES

Aberle,
1967 "Functional Requisites of a Society"
System Change and Conflict Edited by N. J.
Demerath and R. A. Peterson
New York: The Free Press

Angell, Robert Cooley
1938 Free Society and Moral Crisis
Ann Arbor: The University of Michigan Press

Cogdell, Gaston
1978 "Religion and Moral Education"
The Humanist

Cooley, Charles Horton
1909 Social Organization
New York: Charles Scribner's Sons

Davis, Kingsley
1947 "Final Note on a Case of Extreme Isolation"
American Journal of Sociology 52:5
Chicago: The University of Chicago Press

Derthe, Max C., Louis A. Penner, and Kathleen Ulrich
1973 Observer's Reporting of Shoplifting as a
Function of Thief's Race and Sex
Journal of Social Psychology 94:213-221

Durkheim, Emile
1938 The Rules of Sociological Method,
8th Edition
New York, The Free Press
Toronto: Collier-MacMillan Canada Ltd.

1953 Sociology and Philosophy
New York: Cohen & West

Dunford, Franklin W. and Phillip R. Kunz
1972 "The Neutralization of Religious Dissonance"
Review of Religious Research 15

1980 Encyclopedia Americana
Vol. 1

1981 Encyclopedia of Sociology
Giaford: OPG Reference Publishing, Inc.

England, Lynn J. and Phillip R. Kunz
    1975 "Age Specific Divorce Rates"
    Journal of Marriage and the Family   37

Havighurst, R. J. and H. Taba
    1949 Adolescent Character and Personality
    New York: John Wiley

Hindelang, Michael J.
    1972 Moral Evaluations of Illegal Behaviors
    Unpublished Manuscript

Jarvis, Peter
    1972 Religious Education as a Vehicle for Moral
        Education?
    Journal of Moral Education   2:1
    London: Pemberton

Kirkendall, Lester A.
    1972 "Reflections on Sexual Morality"
    Humanist   32

Kohlberg, Lawrence
    1973 The Development of Children's Orientations
        Toward a Moral Order
    Vita Humana   6:1-2

Lauderdale, Pat
    1976 "Deviance and Moral Boundaries"
    American Sociological Review   4:600-676

Lewin, Kurt
    1948 Resolving Social Fact: Selected Papers on
        Group Dynamics
    New York: Harper & Bros.

Matza, D. and G. Sykes
    1957 Techniques of Neutralization
    American Sociological Review   22:712-719

Mills, C. Wright
    1956 The Power Elite
    New York: Oxford Free Press

Miner, Horace
    1956 Body Ritual Among the Nacirema
    American Anthropologist   58:June

O'Augelli, Anthony R.
    1977 "Moral Reasoning and Premarital Sexual
         Behavior: Toward Reasoning About
         Relationships"
    Journal of Social Issues, Vol. 33

Peck, R. H. and R. J. Havighurst
    1960 The Psychology of Character Development
    New York: John Wiley

Reiss, Albert Jr.
    1973 Social Organization and Moral Development
    Unpublished Manuscript
    Family Research Conference
    Brigham Young University

Riesman, David
    1953 The Lonely Crowd
    New York: Doubleday & Company

Sorokin, Pitirim
    1927 Social Morality
    New York: Harper & Bros.

Spencer, Herbert
    1971 Structure, Function and Evolution
    London: Michael Joseph Ltd.

Thomas, William I. and Dorothy Swaine Thomas
    1928 The Child is America
    New York: Knoff

Thomas, William I.
    1951 Social Behavior and Personality
    New York: Social Science Research Council

Tonnies, Ferdinan
    1940 Fundamental Concepts of Sociology
    New York: American Book Company

Weber, Max
    1947 The Theory of Social and Economic
         Organization
    Edited by Talcott Parsons
    New York: Oxford University Press

Winslow, Robert W.
    1968 Crime in a Free Society
    San Diego: Dickenson Publishing Company, Inc.

Yankelovich, Daniel
    1981 New Rules: Searching for Self-fulfillment
        in a World Turned Upside Down
    Random House

NAME INDEX

SUBJECT INDEX

abortion, 16
absolute morality, 27
accidents, 7
adolescence, 22
biological factor, 47
cassette players, 6
cheating, 33, 51
conflict of interest, 69
concience, 56
constitutionality, 23
continuity, 2
crime, 7
crime wave, 9
delinquent parents, 16
detection of crime, 8
discontinuity, 2
divorce, 11
external sanctions, 63
felony, 9
formal sanctions, 63
functional requisites, 20
gemeinschaft, 2, 40
gesellschaft, 40
humanist, vii
ideal types, 3
immigrants, 35
immorality, 68
intergenerational variance, 64
internalization, 65
isolation of children, 26
jailers, 50
liquor industry, 44
massage parlors, 37
misdemeanor, 9
moral absolutes, 60
moral boundaries, 2
moral fabric, vii
negative sanctions, 63
neutralization of dissonance, 53
nuclear freeze, 38
oil field, 14
organismic society, 19
parents, 4
physiological reductionism, 47
plural marriage, 62
polygyny, 68
positions, 55

prisoners, 50
privileged information
religious values, 36
roles, 55
sabbath, 4
sales in food stores, 68
scams, 1
school, 22
secular, vii
shoplifting, 15
situation, 72
situational morality, 31
social pressure, 36
social system, 20
socialization, 21, 45, 71
structural immorality, 68
structure of organization, 68
swindles, 1
symbolic, 25
system, 19
systems, 54
television, 24
tobacco industry, 44
tradition, 35, 39
transmission, 2, 64
vasectomy, 24
wife-sharing, 62